CLINTON CASH

CASH

A GRAPHIC NOVEL

REGNERY
PUBLISHING
A Division of Salem Media Group

Regnery® is a registered trademark of Salem Communications Holding Corporation

Cataloging-in-Publication data on file with the Library of Congress

ISBN 978-1-62157-545-0

Published in the United States by
Regnery Publishing
A Division of Salem Media Group
300 New Jersey Ave NW
Washington, DC 20001
www.Regnery.com

Manufactured in the United States of America

10 9 8 7 6 5 4 3 2

Books are available in quantity for promotional or premium use. For information on discounts and terms, please visit our website: www.Regnery.com.

Distributed to the trade by
Perseus Distribution
250 West 57th Street
New York, NY 10107

Cover design by Ghost Glyph Studios. Cover Illustration by Sergio Cariello & Color Fusion, Inc.

CLINTON
CASH
A GRAPHIC NOVEL

INSPIRED BY THE BOOK BY
PETER SCHWEIZER

ADAPTED BY
CHUCK DIXON WITH BRETT R. SMITH

ART BY
SERGIO CARIELLO
DON HUDSON
GRAHAM NOLAN
PAUL RIVOCHE
ADDITIONAL INKING BY
ANDY OWENS & ALAN ROBINSON

COLOR ART BY
COLOR FUSION, INC.
ADDITIONAL COLOR ART BY
MATTHEW SWIFT

LETTERING AND BOOK DESIGN BY
TAYLOR ESPOSITO
OF GHOST GLYPH STUDIOS

COVER ART BY
SERGIO CARIELLO & COLOR FUSION, INC.

ALTERNATE COVER ART BY
PAUL RIVOCHE & COLOR FUSION, INC.

EDITOR, PRODUCTION DIRECTOR
& CREATIVE DIRECTOR
BRETT R. SMITH

PUBLISHERS
STEPHEN K. BANNON, DAN FLEUETTE
& LARRY SOLOV

DIRECTOR OF RESEARCH
ERIC EGGERS

THE LINCOLN BEDROOM GOES GLOBAL

THIS IS THE STORY OF HILLARY CLINTON.

I DON'T FEEL NO WAYS TAR'D...

HER HUSBAND BILL.

AND WHAT'S *YOUR* NAME?

THEIR DAUGHTER CHELSEA.

I'M OBSESSED WITH DIARRHEA.

LOTS OF THEIR OLD AND NEW FRIENDS.

VINOD GUPTA

FRANK GIUSTRA

HUMA ABEDIN

CHERYL MILLS

CHERYL SABAN

TERRY McAULIFFE

SIDNEY BLUMENTHAL

AND THE CLINTON FOUNDATION, WHICH ALONG WITH THE CLINTON GLOBAL INITIATIVE OCCUPIES TWO FLOORS IN THIS BUILDING IN MANHATTAN.

THE FOUNDATION GOT ITS START IN THE FINAL YEAR OF BILL'S PRESIDENCY.

THIS ISN'T ABOUT ME. IT'S ABOUT HOW MUCH I CARE.

BILL'S LIBRARY BEGAN RECEIVING DONATIONS IN HIS LAST YEARS IN OFFICE.

INCLUDING, IN 1999, ONE MILLION DOLLARS FROM A MAJOR BEER BREWER.

A FEW WEEKS BEFORE RECEIVING THIS CHECK, THE FEDERAL TRADE COMMISSION DROPPED A BID TO REGULATE BEER ADVERTISING AIMED AT UNDERAGE DRINKERS.

IT GOT FUNDING EVEN AS CLINTON WAS LEAVING OFFICE.

CHA-CHING!

MUCH OF IT CAME FROM INDIVIDUALS RECEIVING PRESIDENTIAL PARDONS.

INCLUDING A PARDON FOR BILLIONAIRE FUGITIVE MARC RICH.

RICH WAS FACING A SENTENCE OF 325 YEARS IN PRISON FOR TAX EVASION (48 MILLION UNPAID) AND FELONIOUS DEALS WITH SOME OF THE WORLD'S WORST DESPOTS.

BUT ONLY AFTER RICH'S EX-WIFE WROTE CHECKS TO HILLARY'S SENATE CAMPAIGN, BILL'S LIBRARY, AND THE DEMOCRATIC PARTY.

AND THE CLINTONS WERE JUST GETTING STARTED.

ONCE LIBERATED FROM THE WHITE HOUSE, THE MONEY COULD BEGIN FLOWING TO THEM IN LARGER AMOUNTS.

BILL HIT THE LECTURE CIRCUIT EARNING OVER ONE HUNDRED MILLION DOLLARS IN SPEAKING FEES IN TWELVE YEARS.

BLAH BLAH CONCERN BLAH BLAH SUSTAINABILITY BLAH BLAH.

HILLARY SUCCESSFULLY RAN FOR A SENATE SEAT IN NEW YORK.

AND IT IS A VOTE THAT SAYS TO SADDAM HUSSEIN--THIS IS YOUR LAST CHANCE-- DISARM OR *BE* DISARMED.

WITH HILLARY'S RISE IN POSITION, BILL'S SPEAKING FEES ROSE AS WELL.

AUTOGRA~ 5K
~1K~ 5K
PHOTO OP
~75K~ 100K
HANDSHAKE
~25K~ 50K
SPEECH

AS SENATOR, HILLARY GAINED INFLUENCE AND POWER, ESPECIALLY ON MATTERS CONCERNING FOREIGN POLICY.

BONJOUR.   مرحبا   您好

ЗДРАВСТВУЙТЕ

नमस्ते

AT THE SAME TIME, DONATIONS TO THE CLINTON FOUNDATION, AS WELL AS BILL'S SPEAKING FEES, INCREASINGLY CAME FROM OVERSEAS SOURCES.

MERCI!   شكراً!   谢谢!
СПАСИБО!
धन्यवाद!

IN 2008, PRESIDENT OBAMA PUT HILLARY'S NAME OUT THERE FOR SECRETARY OF STATE.

BLAH BLAH HILLARY CLINTON BLAH BLAH BLAH FOREIGN POLICY BLAH BLAH BLAH...

CHA-CHING!

CONCERNS WERE RAISED ABOUT CONFLICTS OF INTEREST.

ULTIMATELY, THERE IS NO CONFLICT BETWEEN THE FOREIGN POLICY OF THE UNITED STATES AND THE EFFORTS OF THE CLINTON FOUNDATION SEEKING TO REDUCE HUMAN SUFFERING.

THE OBAMA ADMINISTRATION WAS NERVOUS ON THE SUBJECT OF FOREIGN FUNDS.

BOTH CLINTONS OFFERED GUARANTEES.

WE'LL PUBLISH THE LIST OF FOREIGN DONORS ANNUALLY.

AND ALL NEW DONORS WILL BE SCRUTINIZED BY ETHICS OFFICERS.

IT ALL WILL BE PUBLIC AND COMPLETELY TRANSPARENT.

BUT THOSE PROMISES PROVED TO BE FLEETING.

IN ADDITION TO BILL'S SPEAKING FEES RISING SHARPLY, MILLIONS OF DOLLARS IN GIFTS FROM FOREIGN ENTITIES AND BUSINESSES WERE NOT DISCLOSED.

AUTOGRAPH
~~5K~~ 15K
PHOTO OP
~~100K~~ 150K
HANDSHAKE
~~50K~~ 100K
SPEECH

THESE SAME DONORS WERE OFTEN GOVERNMENTS AND CORPORATIONS WHO NEEDED HILLARY'S HELP AS SECRETARY OF STATE TO APPROVE TRANSACTIONS WITH SERIOUS NATIONAL SECURITY IMPLICATIONS.

BUT HOW DID THE CLINTONS AMASS SO MUCH WEALTH IN SUCH A SHORT TIME WITH SO LITTLE OVERSIGHT?

FOR ONE THING, THE CLINTONS OPERATED AT THE FRINGES OF THE DEVELOPED WORLD.

OFTEN APPEARING TO ASSIST IN FACILITATING HUGE RESOURCE EXTRACTION DEALS WORTH HUNDREDS OF MILLIONS.

PROFITS WERE THERE TO BE MADE. PROFITS NOT SEEN SINCE THE HEIGHT OF 19TH CENTURY COLONIALISM.

THE ERA OF GLOBALIZATION WAS HERE, OPENING UP A BONANZA IN DESPOTIC AREAS OF THE DEVELOPING WORLD WHERE THE RULES ARE MORE NEGOTIABLE.

IN THESE CORNERS OF THE GLOBE CORRUPTION AND PAYOFFS ARE SIMPLY PART OF DOING BUSINESS.

AND WE SEE A PATTERN OF FINANCIAL TRANSACTIONS INVOLVING THE CLINTONS THAT OCCURRED CONTEMPORANEOUSLY WITH FAVORABLE U.S. POLICY DECISIONS BENEFITING THOSE DONORS.

SUPPORTERS AND OPPONENTS HAVE CALLED THE CLINTONS MANY THINGS OVER THE YEARS.

BUT ONE WORD YOU NEVER HEAR IS NAÏVE.

A PATTERN OF BEHAVIOR ESTABLISHED ITSELF.

BILL WOULD ARRIVE IN A THIRD WORLD OR DEVELOPING NATION WITH A 'CLOSE FRIEND.'

HELLO, KAZAKHSTAN!

FRANK GIUSTRA.

PHOTO OPS AND LOTS OF SMILES WITH THE FORMER PRESIDENT, HUMANITARIAN, WORLD-RECOGNIZED WISE MAN.

IF THERE'S ANY LITTLE THING I CAN DO FOR YOU, MY FRIEND.

BILL'S TRAVELING BUDDY WOULD JUST HAPPEN TO HAVE BUSINESS INTERESTS PENDING IN THESE COUNTRIES.

WITH ANNUAL YIELD OF ONE POINT FIVE TONS FOR EACH METRIC TON OF ORE...

MEANWHILE, BUREAUCRATIC OR LEGISLATIVE OBSTACLES WERE MYSTERIOUSLY CLEARED OR APPROVALS GRANTED WITHIN THE PURVIEW OF HIS WIFE.

APPROVED!

NEXT!

DONATIONS FROM THE RECENTLY VISITED COUNTRY THEN FLOWED INTO THE CLINTON FOUNDATION.

I DO NOT KNOW! TAKE IT FROM THE CHILDREN'S EDUCATION FUND! DO NOT TROUBLE ME!

AND BILL CLINTON WOULD RECEIVE INVITATIONS TO RETURN TO THE SAME COUNTRY FOR SPEAKING ENGAGEMENTS PAID FOR WITH INFLATED FEES.

BLAH. BLAH. GLOBALIZATION. BLAH, BLAH. ALTERNATE ENERGY SOURCES. BLAH. BLAH.

PERHAPS YOU KNOW THE COUNTRY OF KAZAKHSTAN FROM A POPULAR MOVIE.

IS NICE! HIGH FIVE!

BUT THE NATION OF FIFTEEN MILLION PLAYS A ROLE IN THE REMARKABLE FORTUNES OF THE CLINTONS.

NURSULTAN NAZARBAYEV HAS BEEN PRESIDENT OF KAZAKHSTAN SINCE IT BROKE FROM THE SOVIET UNION IN 1990.

KAZAKHSTAN DOESN'T HAVE ELECTIONS IN THE USUAL SENSE.

NAZARBAYEV REGULARLY WINS RE-ELECTION BY 90%. IN THE MOST RECENT ELECTION, EVEN HIS OPPONENTS CLAIMED THEY VOTED FOR HIM.

NAZARBAYEV!

IS NICE!

HIGH FIVE!

LACKING A MALE HEIR, NAZARBAYEV IMPREGNATED MISS KAZAKHSTAN WHO GAVE BIRTH TO SULTANCHIK.

PROBLEM SOLVED.

IT'S A BOY!

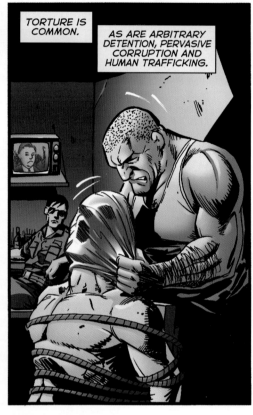

TORTURE IS COMMON.

AS ARE ARBITRARY DETENTION, PERVASIVE CORRUPTION AND HUMAN TRAFFICKING.

SO WHAT PRESSING CONCERN BROUGHT BILL CLINTON TO KAZAKHSTAN?

THE SCOURGE OF HIV/ AIDS.

YET, ACCORDING TO THE WORLD HEALTH ORGANIZATION, THE INCIDENCE OF AIDS IN KAZAKHSTAN IS NEAR STATISTICAL ZERO.

WHY NOT LEND THE CLINTON FOUNDATION'S HELP TO A NATION MORE AFFECTED BY THE DISEASE?

24.1%

0.1%

Kazakhstan   Botswana

WHY WOULD BILL CLINTON BESTOW AN AIR OF RESPECTABILITY TO A BACKWATER BILLIONAIRE WITH A TREACHEROUS HUMAN RIGHTS RECORD?

FRANK GIUSTRA

BILL WAS FLOWN IN ON A JET BELONGING TO FRANK GIUSTRA, A CANADIAN CAPITALIST, WHO HAD A KEEN INTEREST IN THE NATURAL RESOURCES OF THE COUNTRY.

ALL MY CHIPS ARE ON BILL CLINTON. HE'S A WORLDWIDE BRAND AND HE CAN **DO** THINGS AND **ASK** FOR THINGS THAT NO ONE ELSE CAN.*

*THE NEW YORKER, 9-18-2006.

GIUSTRA OWNED A COMPANY CALLED URASIA.

IT WAS A SHELL COMPANY AND FAR FROM THE LOGICAL CHOICE FOR LUCRATIVE MINING CONTRACTS IN THE SOON-TO-BE-BOOMING KAZAKHSTAN.

AND THE SUBJECT OF THESE HOTLY SOUGHT MINING CONTRACTS?

URANIUM.

KAZAKHSTAN SITS ON THE WORLD'S RICHEST DEPOSITS OF THE RADIOACTIVE ORE.

WHEN KAZATOMPROM, THE COUNTRY'S NATIONAL MINING AUTHORITY, DRAGGED THEIR FEET ON AWARDING GIUSTRA THE CONTRACTS--

--A MEETING BETWEEN KAZAKHI PRIME MINISTER MASSIMOV AND THEN-SENATOR HILLARY CLINTON WAS CANCELLED.

HONORABLE HILLARY RODHAM CLINTON UNITED STATES SENATOR

REASON OFFERED?

SHE **WON'T** SEE YOU UNTIL KAZAKH OFFICIALS **APPROVE** THE GIUSTRA URANIUM DEAL.

OH.

AT STAKE WAS HUNDREDS OF MILLIONS IN FOREIGN AID FROM THE USA.

MOUKHTAR DZHAKISHEV, HEAD OF KAZATOMPRON, WAS LATER A GUEST AT THE CLINTON HOME IN CHAPPAQUA TO DISCUSS THE BROADER URANIUM MARKET IN KAZAKHSTAN.

BILL DID HIS PART BY PRAISING PRESIDENT NAZARBAYEV FOR--

--OPENING UP THE SOCIAL AND POLITICAL LIFE OF YOUR COUNTRY.

AND I BELIEVE THAT KAZAKHSTAN SHOULD HEAD THE ORGANIZATION FOR SECURITY AND COOPERATION IN EUROPE TO AID THEM WITH THEIR FINE WORK SECURING HUMAN RIGHTS FOR ALL.

IS NICE.

IN 2004, AS COMMISSIONER OF THE COMMISSION ON SECURITY AND COOPERATION IN EUROPE, HILLARY CO-SIGNED A LETTER TO THE STATE DEPARTMENT STATING THAT KAZAKHSTAN'S BID TO HEAD UP THE OSCE WOULD NOT BE ACCEPTABLE--

--BECAUSE OF ITS RECORD ON HUMAN RIGHTS.

IN 2008, HEARINGS WERE HELD BY THE SAME COMMISSION ON THE SUBJECT OF KAZAKHSTAN'S PROPOSED CHAIRMANSHIP OF THE OSCE.

SEN. HILLARY CLINTON

HILLARY DID NOT SHOW UP FOR THE HEARINGS.

FRANK GIUSTRA, TO THE SHOCK OF THE GLOBAL MINING INDUSTRY, WAS AWARDED A 30% STAKE IN THE KHARASSAN URANIUM PROJECT AND 70% OF THE BETPAK-DALA PROJECT.

GIUSTRA'S COMPANY, URASIA WAS NOW A MAJOR URANIUM PRODUCER WHEN IT HADN'T EVEN EXISTED A FEW MONTHS BEFORE.

IN THE MONTHS THAT FOLLOWED, GIUSTRA GAVE THE CLINTON FOUNDATION 31.3 MILLION DOLLARS.

The Clinton Foundation $31,000,000
THIRTY-ONE MILLION
CONGRATULATIONS

IT WOULD BE THE FIRST OF **MANY** LARGE DONATIONS.

PRESSURE WAS MOUNTING IN WASHINGTON OVER NAZARBAYEV'S HUMAN RIGHTS RECORD.

IF THIS CLOWN DOESN'T CLEAN UP HIS ACT I'M **NOT** SIGNING OFF ON THIS CRAP!

2008.

UNLESS VISIBLE PROGRESS IS ATTAINED QUICKLY, I WILL NOT BE ABLE TO SUPPORT KAZAKHSTAN IN ITS QUEST TO ASSUME CHAIRMANSHIP OF THE OSCE.

JOE BIDEN

2010.

WHEN THE DEBATE REACHED THE SENATE HILLARY WAS NOW STRANGELY SILENT ON THE SUBJECT.

Sen. Hillary Clinton

BILL HOSTED THE DICTATOR IN NEW YORK WHERE HE ATTENDED A MEETING OF THE CLINTON GLOBAL INITIATIVE.

TWO MONTHS LATER, NAZARBAYEV WAS AWARDED THE **OSCE** CHAIR.

IS NICE!

HIGH FIVE!

URASIA WOULD MERGE WITH CANADIAN FIRM URANIUM ONE WITH FRANK GIUSTRA AND PARTNERS OWNING 60% OF THE STOCK.

GIUSTRA WOULD ANNOUNCE A FUTURE GIFT OF 100 MILLION DOLLARS TO THE CLINTON FOUNDATION ALONG WITH A SHARE OF HIS PROFITS.

COMMITMENTS AND DONATIONS FROM INVESTORS WHO PROFITED FROM THE KAZAKHI DEAL EXCEEDED 145 MILLION DOLLARS.

I'M PROUD OF YOU GUYS.

BILL CLINTON HAILED THE WINDFALL AS A SELFLESS PHILANTHROPIC GESTURE.

DON'T BE STRANGERS, Y'ALL!

A GROUP OF CANADIAN INVESTORS JUST HAPPENED TO BECOME CONSPICUOUSLY LARGE CONTRIBUTORS TO THE CLINTON FOUNDATION OVER A VERY SHORT PERIOD OF TIME.

GIUSTRA WENT FURTHER THAN JUST MONETARY REMUNERATIONS. HE ALSO HELD SEVERAL CELEBRITY-STUDDED PARTIES FOR BILL.

THE CLINTONS' ACTIONS COULD NOT BE JUSTIFIED USING THE USUAL POLITICIAN'S DODGE THAT THEY WERE CREATING JOBS FOR AMERICANS.

IT HAD THE APPEARANCE OF A STRAIGHT QUID PRO QUO. THE HELP OF A FORMER PRESIDENT AND CURRENT US SENATOR IN EXCHANGE FOR HEFTY DONATIONS AND GIFTS.

BUT THE INTERNATIONAL SCOPE OF THE DEALS WOULD EXPAND BEYOND KAZAKHSTAN, CANADA, WASHINGTON, AND CHAPPAQUA.

THE FLOW OF MONEY WOULD SOON INCREASE.

HAITI

A YEAR FOLLOWING THE EARTH-QUAKE IN HAITI, MILLIONS ARE HOMELESS AND LIVING IN SQUALID LEAN-TOS AND SHEDS.

PROMISED AID IS SLOW IN COMING AND IN INSUFFICIENT AMOUNTS.

WILL THERE BE ENOUGH, PAPA?

I DO NOT KNOW, *PITIT GASON.*

WE DID NOT GET ANYTHING YESTERDAY.

LAST ONE!

NON!

STAY CLOSE, *TIMOUN!* DO NOT BE FRIGHTENED!

UH!

PAPA!

I AM ALL RIGHT! IT IS ONLY A BUMP!

WE WILL BE FINE. THESE THINGS TAKE TIME. THERE WILL SOON BE FOOD FOR YOU. A JOB FOR ME.

AND A HOUSE?

YES, A HOUSE.

A BETTER PLACE THAN WE HAVE EVER LIVED. WITH CLEAN WATER AND SUN-LIGHT AND A YARD.

THESE THINGS TAKE TIME, YOU KNOW.

WHEN, PAPA?

SOON.

NOUVELLES MAISONS BIENTÔT!

2010 2011

SOON.

HILLDRY'S RE-SET

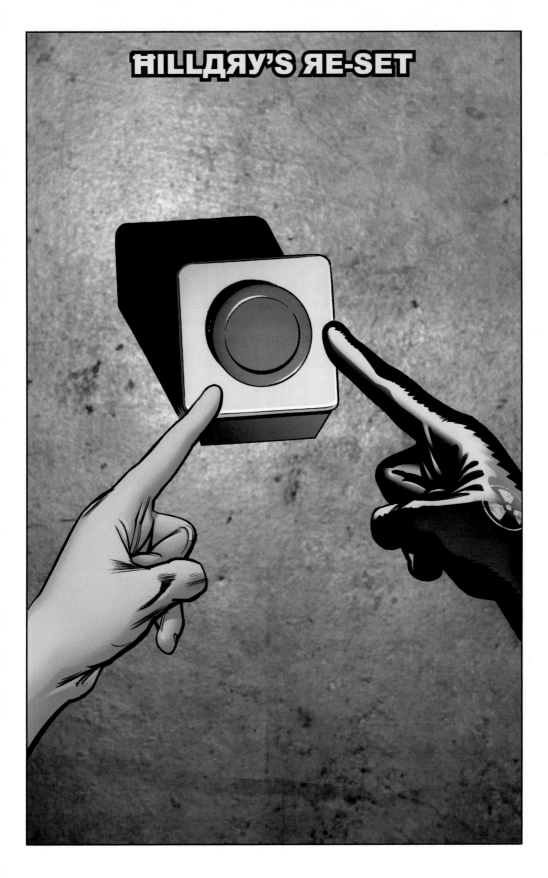

GEORGE W. BUSH HAD HIS OWN OPINION OF RUSSIAN PRESIDENT VLADIMIR PUTIN.

I WAS ABLE TO GET A SENSE OF HIS SOUL.

AND HILLARY CLINTON HAD HER OWN.

PUTIN DOESN'T HAVE A SOUL.

IT'S IMPORTANT IN RUSSIA TO GET THE LAST WORD.

AT A MINIMUM, A HEAD OF STATE SHOULD HAVE A HEAD.

AS SECRETARY OF STATE, HILLARY WAS DETERMINED TO 'START OVER' WITH RUSSIA, WIPING THE SLATE CLEAN BETWEEN THE TWO COUNTRIES.

WHAT IS?

IT'S A RE-SET BUTTON! HA HA HA HA!

IS STUPID, NO?

RUSSIAN FOREIGN MINISTER SERGEY LAVROV

THIS SPIRIT OF FORGIVENESS AND NEW BEGINNINGS FROM THE OBAMA ADMINISTRATION THROUGH HILLARY WAS WELCOME IN THE KREMLIN.

IT FIT INTO THE RUSSIAN GOVERNMENT'S PLANS TO EXPAND THEIR GLOBAL ECONOMIC REACH.

CENTRAL TO RUSSIA'S STRATEGY?

NUCLEAR ENERGY.

WITH THE ENTIRE RUSSIAN NUCLEAR INDUSTRY, FROM MINING TO POWER GENERATION TO NUCLEAR WEAPONS, UNDER THE CONTROL OF ONE HIGHLY SECRETIVE GOVERNMENT AGENCY.

ROSATOM

ROSATOM.

THE LONGTIME HEAD OF ROSATOM IS SERGEI KIRIYENKO.

A TECHNOCRAT WHOSE CAREER BEGAN IN THE WANING DAYS OF THE SOVIET UNION.

UNDER HIS AEGIS, ROSATOM BUILT THE INFAMOUS BUSHEHR NUCLEAR REACTORS IN IRAN.

WE NEED THESE PLANTS FOR THE PEACEFUL GENERATION OF POWER FOR THE IRANIAN PEOPLE.

NOT FOR PLUTONIUM FOR SCOURING THE HATED JEWS OFF THE PLANET.

ROSATOM ALSO DOES BUSINESS IN NORTH KOREA, VENEZUELA AND MYANMAR.

BUT IN ORDER TO FEED THE ENORMOUS DEMAND FOR URANIUM THAT THEIR PLANS REQUIRE, ROSATOM AND THE RUSSIAN HEIRARCHY TURN TO INTERNATIONAL SOURCES FOR THE ELEMENT.

THEY SET THEIR SIGHTS ON A CANADIAN COMPANY WE'RE FAMILIAR WITH BY NOW.

uranium one™
investing in our energy

AND WHO JUST HAPPENED TO BE DIRECTING NEGOTIATIONS WITH THE RUSSIANS CONCERNING CIVILIAN NUCLEAR ENERGY?

2010

SLADKIY PRIVET ACEM, MOI GOLUB!*

*SWEET HELLOS TO EVERYONE, MY PIGEONS!

HILLARY'S MEETING WITH PUTIN WAS OFFICIALLY OVER MOSCOW'S PLANS TO BUILD MORE NUCLEAR POWER STATIONS IN IRAN.

WE ARE BEING 'ALL IN.'

THIS CAME AT A TIME WHEN MOSCOW WAS SEEKING NEW URANIUM RESERVES THROUGH PURCHASES BY ROSATOM.

SPECIFICALLY, THE RUSSIANS WANTED TO SIGNIFICANTLY INCREASE THEIR SHARE HOLDINGS IN URANIUM ONE INCLUDING OPERATIONS INSIDE THE UNITED STATES.

GRAND CANYON NATIONAL PARK

uraniumone™
investing in our energy

COMING SOON!

ROSATOM WAS OFFERING A TOTAL BUY-OUT OF THE COMPANY'S SHAREHOLDERS.

SWEETENING THE DEAL WITH A ONE-DOLLAR A SHARE CASH BONUS.

BUT APPROVAL OF SUCH A DEAL FELL TO CFIUS.*

A SECRETIVE EXECUTIVE BRANCH TASK FORCE THAT OVERSEES INVESTMENT TRANSACTIONS THAT DIRECTLY AFFECT AMERICAN NATIONAL SECURITY.

*CFIUS: COMMITTEE ON FOREIGN INVESTMENT IN THE UNITED STATES.

MEMBERS OF THAT COMMITTEE INCLUDED THE SECRETARY OF STATE.

WHAT COULD IT HURT?

AMONG THOSE WITH AN INTEREST IN THE SALE WAS IAN TELFER, FORMER CHAIRMAN OF THE WORLED GOLD COUNCIL AND CURRENT CHAIRMAN OF URANIUM ONE.

TELFER BEGAN FUNNELING PAYMENTS TO THE CLINTON FOUNDATION THROUGH A CANADIAN ENTITY CALLED THE FERNWOOD FOUNDATION.

HIS CONTRIBUTIONS WOULD TOTAL 2.35 MILLION DOLLARS.

THESE TRANFERS WOULD NOT APPEAR IN CLINTON FOUNDATION STATEMENTS.

ANOTHER 2.6 MILLION FOUND ITS WAY TO THE CLINTON FOUNDATION THROUGH ANOTHER CANADIAN OUTFIT CALLED SALIDA CAPITAL.

ANOTHER COMPANY WITH THE SAME NAME WOULD BE IDENTIFIED AS A WHOLLY-OWNED SUBSIDIARY OF THE RUSSIAN STATE NUCLEAR AGENCY.

Salida Capital

OTHER OFFICERS, ADVISORS AND INVESTORS AT URANIUM ONE WERE ALSO MAJOR CONTRIBUTORS AND POSITION HOLDERS AT THE CLINTON FOUNDATION.

uranium
investing in our energy

CLINTON FOUNDATION

AS THE DEAL TO SELL URANIUM ONE SAT ON THE TABLE, RENAISSANCE CAPITAL PAID BILL CLINTON A RECORD HALF MILLION DOLLARS FOR A ONE HOUR SPEECH.

REGISTERED IN CYPRUS, RENCAP WAS HEADED UP BY KREMLIN OFFICIALS AND MEMBERS OF THE RUSSIAN INTELLIGENCE SERVICE.

HILLARY'S OPPOSITION WOULD HAVE BEEN ENOUGH TO ALL BUT STOP THE DEAL.

THAT NEVER HAPPENED.

THE DEAL GIVES ROSATOM CONTROLLING STOCK IN THE LARGEST URANIUM MINING OPERATION IN NORTH AMERICA.

KHAZAKI PRIME MINISTER MUKHTAR DZHAKISHEV BELIEVED THAT CLINTON PAL FRANK GIUSTRA MADE 300 MILLION ON THE SALE.

RUSSIAN MEDIA WAS ECSTATIC ANNOUNCING THAT ROSTAOM HAD CORNERED THE WORLD URANIUM MARKET.

UNDER THE RE-SET, PRAVDA HAILED: 'RUSSIAN NUCLEAR ENERGY CONQUERS THE WORLD'.

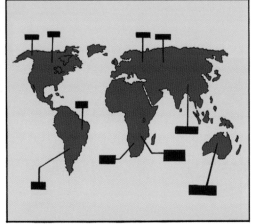

ROSATOM BEGAN CONSTRUCTION A SECOND NUCLEAR PLANT AT BUSHEHR.

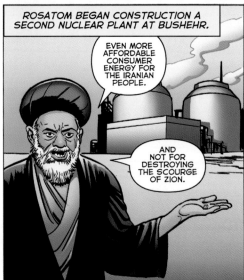

EVEN MORE AFFORDABLE CONSUMER ENERGY FOR THE IRANIAN PEOPLE.

AND NOT FOR DESTROYING THE SCOURGE OF ZION.

AFTER A LONG RECORD OF OPPOSING SUCH DEALS, HILLARY DIDN'T OBJECT.

COULD IT BE BECAUSE SHAREHOLDERS INVOLVED IN THE TRANSACTIONS HAD TRANSFERRED NEARLY 145 MILLION DOLLARS TO THE CLINTON FOUNDATION?

TRANSFERS THAT WERE NEVER REVEALED TO HER COLLEAGUES, THE WHITE HOUSE OR CAPITOL HILL.

जो झूठ
गंदा सौदा
अव
UA
बंबई पैलेस उत्पादन
भारत के परमाणु
A BOMBAY PALACE PRODUCTION
(INDIA'S NUKES)
बिल क्लिंटन
हिलेरी क्लिंटन

MAY, 1998.

OPERATION SHAKTI, AN INDIAN ARMY PROGRAM, DEPLOYS A SERIES OF UNDERGROUND NUCLEAR TESTS.

OVERNIGHT, INDIA BECOMES A NUCLEAR POWER.

ALL OF WHICH COMES AS AN UNPLEASANT SURPISE TO THEN-PRESIDENT BILL CLINTON.

PSST... PSST...

WHAT THE--?

HE SWIFTLY CONDEMNS THE GOVERNMENT IN NEW DELHI AND IMPOSES SANCTIONS ON INDIA.

INDIA RISKS INTERNATIONAL ISOLATION UNLESS THEY TAKE STEPS TO REDUCE NUCLEAR DANGERS.

AS A SENATOR AND PRESIDENTIAL CANDIDATE, HILLARY ALSO MADE HER DISPLEASURE KNOWN.

THEY DID A VERY, VERY, VERY BAD THING AND I'M VERY PISSED AT THEM.

AS PRESIDENT, I WILL SUPPORT EFFORTS TO SUPPLEMENT THE NUCLEAR PROLIFERATION TREATY.

THE INDIAN GOVERNMENT SOUGHT WAYS TO REGAIN THE FAVOR OF THE CLINTONS.

THROUGH CONTRIBUTIONS TO HILLARY'S CAMPAIGNS.

AND LUCRATIVE SPEAKING FEES FOR BILL.

AND DONATIONS TO THE CLINTON FOUNDATION.

SANT CHATWAL IS A SIKH, FORMER MILITARY JET PILOT AND OWNER OF THE BOMBAY PALACE RESTAURANT AND HAMPSHIRE HOTEL CHAIN.

HE IS ALSO A HEAVY DONOR TO DEMOCRATIC PARTY CANDIDATES.

IN THE 1990s THE IRS CLAIMED HE OWED 30 MILLION IN UNPAID TAXES. THE FDIC CLAIMED UNPAID LOANS IN EXCESS OF 12 MILLION.

DESPITE HIS MONEY WOES HE WAS ABLE TO THROW A LAVISH FUNDRAISER FOR HILLARY CLINTON'S SENATE CAMPAIGN.

A FEW MONTHS LATER THE FEDERAL CASES AGAINST CHATWAL WERE ABRUPTLY SETTLED.

HE MADE A PAYMENT OF $125,000 AND WALKED AWAY WITH A CLEAN RECORD.

HE ALSO ATTENDED CHELSEA'S WEDDING AS A GUEST.

AN INVITATION GRANTED TO ONLY THE CLOSEST OF THE CLINTON INSIDERS.

IN ADDITION TO USING POLITICAL FAVORS TO EXTRICATE HIM FROM FEDERAL PROSECUTION--

CHATWAL HAS CANDIDLY ADMITTED TO SPENDING MONEY, TIME, AND EFFORT TO MAKE SURE THAT INDIA IS DEALT WITH FAVORABLY ON NUCLEAR MATTERS.

CHATWAL'S SON VIKRAM WAS ALSO A CLINTON BENEFACTOR.

HE BECAME HILLARY'S 2008 CAMPAIGN BUNDLER.

FAMOUS FOR DATING ACTRESSES AND SUPERMODELS, VIKRAM WAS KNOWN AROUND MANHATTAN AS THE 'TURBAN COWBOY.'

HE CONSIDERED HIMSELF TO BE A CLOSE FRIEND OF THE CLINTONS.

HA HA HA HA!

YOU ARE CRACKING ME UP, BILL!

IN HIS OWN WORDS:

I KNOW [BILL CLINTON] VERY WELL.

WE TALK OF WOMEN AND MODELS I'VE DATED. HE, LIKE ANY MAN IN THE WORLD, APPRECIATES BEAUTY.

BILL CLINTON EVEN ATTENDED VIKRAM'S WEDDING.

AN EXTRAVAGANZA FEATURING WHITE-PAINTED ELEPHANTS AND DANCING EUNUCHS.

GEORGE W. BUSH AND THE INDIAN PRIME MINISTER SIGN A LETTER OF INTENT TO ALLOW INDIA ACCESS TO US NUCLEAR TECHNOLOGY.

2005.

IT IS THE END OF INDIA'S NUCLEAR APARTHEID.

YOU BET.

HILLARY CLINTON SITS ON THE SENATE-ARMED SERVICES COMMITTEE AS WELL AS THE SUBCOMMITTEE ON EMERGING THREATS AND CAPABILITIES.

SHE WAS NOW REMARKABLY SILENT ON THE ISSUE OF COOPERATION WITH INDIA ON NUCLEAR MATTERS.

IN THE SAME YEAR, BILL ARRIVED IN LUCKNOW, INDIA. HE WAS ESCORTED BY SANT CHATWAL.

ALONG FOR THE RIDE?

FRANK GIUSTRA.

BILL AND HIS SIX-PERSON DELEGATION WAS GIVEN TWO FLOORS IN THE PALATIAL TAJ HOTEL.

THEY WERE ENTERTAINED AT A FEAST THAT EVENING.

IT'S THERE THAT BILL FIRST MET AMAR SINGH, A MEMBER OF THE INDIAN PARLIAMENT.

SINGH'S ACCESS TO BIG MONEY WAS 'LEGENDARY', ACCORDING TO THE INDIAN PRESS.

BILL AND SINGH IMMEDIATELY BECAME FRIENDS AND SINGH WAS ELEVATED IN THE WORLD OF THE CLINTONS.

HE WOULD SIT AT THE HEAD TABLE OF THE CLINTON GLOBAL INITIATIVE AND BE A FREQUENT HOUSE GUEST IN CHAPPAQUA.

HILLARY'S CLOSEST ADVISORS WERE DEAD SET AGAINST ANY KIND OF DEAL.

THE UNITED STATES RECEIVED NOTHING IN THE FORM OF CONCRETE INDIAN STEPS TOWARD NUCLEAR RESTRAINT IN ITS MILITARY PROGRAMS.

STROBE TALBOTT, FORMERLY OF BILL CLINTON'S STATE DEPARTMENT.

A RADICAL DEPARTURE FROM LONGSTANDING LEGAL OBLIGATIONS AND POLICIES THAT PRECLUDED NUCLEAR COOPERATION WITH STATES NOT PARTY TO THE NONPROLIFERATION TREATY.

ROBERT EINHORN, HILLARY'S NUCLEAR PROLIFERATION ADVISER.

THE NUCLEAR NONPROLIFERATION TREATY WOULD BE SHREDDED AND INDIA'S YEARLY PRODUCTION CAPABILITY WOULD LIKELY INCREASE FROM SEVEN BOMBS TO FORTY OR FIFTY.

ELLEN TAUSCHER, US CONGRESSWOMAN.

STILL, HILLARY REMAINED UNDECIDED.

♪ I DUNNO...

A CORE GROUP OF INDIAN POLITICIANS AND MONEY MEN TASKED AMAR SINGH TO CLOSE THE DEAL.

HE ARRIVED IN NEW YORK IN LATE SEPTEMBER 2008.

HE MET WITH HILLARY CLINTON PRIVATELY AT A DINNER THAT LASTED TWO HOURS.

BACK IN INDIA, SINGH IS CONFIDENT THE DEAL WILL GO INDIA'S WAY.

HAS SENATOR HILLARY CLINTON PROMISED ALL THE SUPPORT TO PASS THE BILL THROUGH CONGRESS?

YES. BECAUSE OF THE CLINTONS I AM CLOSE TO THE DEMOCRATS.

WE'LL BLOCK THE DAMN VOTE.

WE CAN'T ALLOW AN IMBALANCE OF NUCLEAR CAPABILITY IN THE REGION.

WHO THE HELL DOES SHE THINK SHE IS?

WHAT'S IN IT FOR US?

HILLARY'S POSITION ON THE SUBJECT OF THE PROLIFERATION OF NUCLEAR WEAPONS HAD EVOLVED.

1967.

NO MORE NUKES! NO MORE NUKES!

2005.

I FERVENTLY SUPPORT THE NON-PROLIFERATION TREATY AND THE NUCLEAR TEST BAN TREATY.

2008.

AS PRESIDENT, I WILL SUPPORT EFFORTS TO SUPPLEMENT THE NPT!

2009.

WE MUST REINVIGORATE OUR COMMITMENT TO THE NPT IN ORDER TO PREVENT THE SPREAD OF NUCLEAR WEAPONS AND THE POTENTIAL FOR NUCLEAR TERRORISM.

NO MORE NUKES! NO MORE NUKES!

THE BILL PASSED WITHOUT BLOCKAGE OR AMENDMENT.

SANCTIONS WERE LIFTED.

INDIA WAS ALLOWED TO PURCHASE FISSIONABLE MATERIALS BOTH FOR POWER GENERATION AND WEAPONS.

ALL *WITHOUT* BECOMING A SIGNEE OF THE NON-PROLIFERATION TREATY.

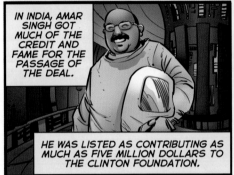

IN INDIA, AMAR SINGH GOT MUCH OF THE CREDIT AND FAME FOR THE PASSAGE OF THE DEAL.

HE WAS LISTED AS CONTRIBUTING AS MUCH AS FIVE MILLION DOLLARS TO THE CLINTON FOUNDATION.

THE ONLY TROUBLE WAS THAT SINGH'S ENTIRE NET WORTH WAS FIVE MILLION DOLLARS.

YOU GAVE AWAY ALL OF YOUR MONEY?

NO!

THEN WHERE DID THE MONEY COME FROM?

I HAVE NO MORE TO SAY!

IN SPITE OF UNANSWERED QUESTIONS ABOUT HIS FINANCES, CHATWAL WAS AWARDED THE PADMA BHUSHAN AWARD, ONE OF HIS COUNTRY'S MOST PRESTIGIOUS HONORS.

IT WAS WIDELY UNDERSTOOD HOW HE EARNED THE PRIZE.

CHATWAL HAD GOTTEN CLOSE TO THE CLINTONS.

IN SANT CHATWAL'S OWN WORDS:

EVEN MY CLOSE FRIEND HILLARY CLINTON WAS NOT IN FAVOR OF THE DEAL.

IN POLITICS, NOTHING COMES FREE. YOU HAVE TO WRITE CHECKS IN THE AMERICAN POLITICAL SYSTEM.

AMAR SINGH WAS ARRESTED FOR BRIBING THREE FELLOW MEMBERS OF PARLIAMENT.

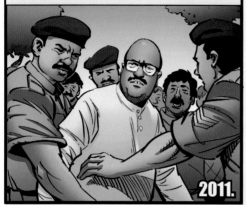

2011.

THE TURBAN COWBOY WAS ARRESTED IN A FLORIDA AIRPORT ON HEROIN AND COCAINE CHARGES.

2013.

2014.

AND KARMA OR THE LAW EVEN CAUGHT UP WITH SANT CHATWAL AS HE PLED GUILTY IN FEDERAL COURT FOR MAKING ILLEGAL CAMPAIGN CONTRIBUTIONS.

INCLUDING ONES TO HILLARY CLINTON'S SENATE AND PRESIDENTIAL CAMPAIGNS.

WITHOUT CASH NOBODY WILL EVEN **TALK** TO YOU.

THAT'S THE **ONLY** WAY TO BUY THEM.

THE CLINTONS HAVE NEVER EXPLAINED WHO DONATED THE MILLIONS THE FOUNDATION ATTRIBUTED TO AMAR SINGH.

OR DISCUSSED THE ROLE SANT CHATWAL PLAYED IN CHANGING HILLARY'S POSITION.

AND SINCE HIS ADMISSION OF GUILT, THE FOUNDATION HAS ERASED ANY MENTION OF HIM FROM THEIR WEBSITE.

HAITI

OVER TWO YEARS AFTER THE CATASTROPHIC QUAKE, LIFE IN HAITI IS STILL ABOUT LINES.

LINES FOR MEDICAL CARE.

LINES FOR WATER.

LINES FOR WORK.

WHAT ARE THEY SAYING?

PARC INDUSTRIEL DE CARACOL

THEY LOOK ANGRY.

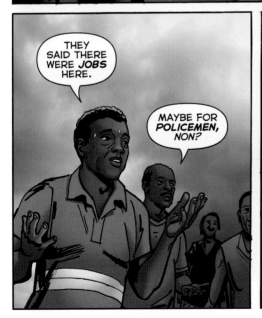

THEY SAID THERE WERE *JOBS* HERE.

MAYBE FOR *POLICEMEN*, NON?

NOTHING *HERE* FOR YOU!

GO *AWAY!* GET *AWAY* FROM HERE!

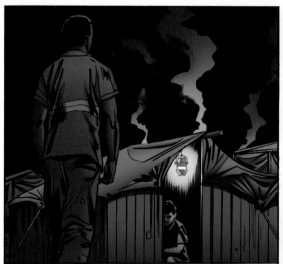

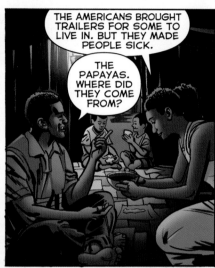

THE AMERICANS BROUGHT TRAILERS FOR SOME TO LIVE IN. BUT THEY MADE PEOPLE SICK.

THE PAPAYAS. WHERE DID THEY COME FROM?

SOMEONE GAVE THEM TO ME.

GAVE? THEM?

IT IS TRUE, PAPA.

NO ONE GAVE THEM TO YOU.

FIRST YOU STEAL AND THEN YOU LIE?

PAPA.

PITIT FI...

I AM SORRY.

OCTOBER, 2011.

🎵 I WANT YOUR DRAMA THE TOUCH OF YOUR HAND I WANT YOUR LEATHER-STUDDED KISS IN THE SAND... 🎵

AN ALL-STAR GALA FOR THE CLINTON FOUNDATION CALLED "A DECADE OF DIFFERENCE."

🎵 LOVE-LOVE-LOVE I WANT YOUR LOVE YOU KNOW THAT I WANT YOU YOU KNOW THAT I NEED YOU 🎵

LADY GAGA REWROTE THE LYRICS OF ONE OF HER HITS TO REFER SPECIFICALLY TO ONE OF THE GUESTS OF HONOR.

🎵 I DON'T WANNA BE FRIENDS. OH-OH-OH-OH-OOOH! 🎵

🎵 WANT YOUR BAD ROMANCE! WANT YOUR BILL ROMANCE! 🎵

THE CLINTON FOUNDATION IS NOT YOUR TYPICAL CHARITY.

MOST CHARITIES DON'T HAVE AN EX-PRESIDENT, AN EX-SECRETARY OF STATE AND THEIR DAUGHTER RUNNING THE SHOW.

FOR ALL THE BENEFITS THAT DERIVE FROM THEIR STAR POWER, THE REAL PROBLEM IS DELINEATING WHERE THE CLINTON POLITICAL MACHINE AND MONEYMAKING VENTURES END--

--AND WHERE THEIR CHARITY BEGINS.

FOUNDED IN 2001, THE FOUNDATION BOASTS A PERMANENT STAFF OF 350.

OUT OF THE FOUNDATION SPRINGS A HYDRA OF PROJECTS.

CLINTON HEALTH ACCESS INITIATIVE. PLEASE HOLD.

CLINTON CLIMATE INITIATIVE. PLEASE HOLD.

CLINTON HUNTER INITIATIVE. PLEASE HOLD.

CLINTON ECONOMIC OPPORTUNITY INITIATIVE. PLEASE HOLD.

CLINTON NO CEILINGS PROJECT. PLEASE HOLD.

CLINTON ALLIANCE FOR A HEALTHIER GENERATION. PLEASE HOLD.

THE CHARITY SERVES AS A CROSSOVER, MELANGE OR GO-BETWEEN WHERE POLITICS, PHILANTHROPY AND BUSINESS CONVERGE.

AS **FORTUNE** MAGAZINE PUT IT, "THE CLINTON FOUNDATION IS A NEW TURN IN PHILANTHROPY IN WHICH THE LINES BETWEEN NOT-FOR-PROFITS, POLITICS AND BUSINESS TEND TO BLUR."

BILL CLINTON HAS SAID AS MUCH HIMSELF.

I BELIEVE THAT IN THE YEARS AHEAD, THE ORGANIZATION AND EXPANSION OF PUBLIC-GOODS MARKETS WILL BECOME ONE OF THE MOST IMPORTANT AREAS OF PHILANTHROPY, AND WILL BE AN AREA WHERE PHILANTHROPY SOMETIMES BLURS INTO STRICT PRIVATE ENTERPRISE.*

*THE ATLANTIC, 10-1-2007

BRINGING TOGETHER BUSINESS, GOVERNMENT AND NGOS IS WHAT BILL CALLS "CONVENING POWER."

WON'T YOU CARE AS MUCH AS I DO?

BEING A CONVENING POWER MEANS THAT THE ORGANIZATION DOESN'T ACTUALLY NEED TO GET ITS HANDS DIRTY.

ICK!

WHEN THE GATES FOUNDATION PROVIDES REVENUE TO THE CLINTON FOUNDATION, THE CLINTONS, IN TURN, BECOME PARTNERS WITH THE GATES IN THEIR INITIATIVES.

BUT WITH LITTLE DIRECT RESPONSIBILITY.

IN THIS WAY, THE FOUNDATION IS ABLE TO TAKE CREDIT FOR GOOD RESULTS AND AVOID BLAME FOR BAD ONES.

IS THIS ALL THAT'S ON?

ANOTHER IMPORTANT FUNCTION OF THE CLINTON FOUNDATION APPEARS TO BE EMPLOYING LONG TIME CLINTON ASSOCIATES.

THE FOUNDATION'S SENIOR RANKS ARE POPULATED WITH CLINTON APPARATCHIKS WITH NO EXPERIENCE IN CHARITABLE WORK.

THE FOUNDATION ALSO HANDS OUT HONORARY TITLES SUCH AS "ADVISOR" TO BUSINESSMEN AND INVESTORS.

THESE AWARDS ARE ADDED TO THE RESUMES OF OPERATORS IN THE DEVELOPING WORLD TO BUILD THEIR CACHET.

THE TIGHTNESS OF THE BOARD'S CRONYISM RANG ALARM BELLS AT PLACES LIKE THE BETTER BUSINESS BUREAU WHO DETERMINED THAT THE FOUNDATION--

--FAILS TO MEET THE MINIMUM STANDARDS OF ACCOUNTABILITY AND TRANSPARENCY.

CHARITY NAVIGATOR, WHICH EVALUATES AND RANKS PHILANTHROPIC GROUPS, WILL NOT RANK OR GRADE THE CLINTON FOUNDATION BECAUSE ITS--

--ATYPICAL BUSINESS MODEL MAKES IT DIFFICULT, IF NOT IMPOSSIBLE, TO EVALUATE.

PERHAPS THE MOST IMPORTANT FUNCTION OF THE FOUNDATIONS IS TO BOLSTER BILL AND HILLARY'S REPUTATIONS AT GLOBAL HUMANITARIANS.

BUT HOW MUCH GOOD HAVE THEY ACTUALLY DONE?

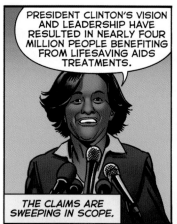

PRESIDENT CLINTON'S VISION AND LEADERSHIP HAVE RESULTED IN NEARLY FOUR MILLION PEOPLE BENEFITING FROM LIFESAVING AIDS TREATMENTS.

THE CLAIMS ARE SWEEPING IN SCOPE.

WE WERE ABLE TO LOWER THE TREATMENT FOR HIV PATIENTS TO JUST UNDER $140 A PERSON A YEAR.

THE FOUNDATION IS NOW INVOLVED IN TREATING OVER TWO-THIRDS OF THE WORLD'S CHILDREN UNDER TREATMENT FOR AIDS.

BUT WHAT EXACTLY DOES "INVOLVED?" MEAN?

THE IMPRESSION IS THAT BILL AND HILLARY ARE ACTUALLY ADMINISTERING DRUGS TO SICK PEOPLE.

EXCEPT THAT THE FOUNDATION DOES NOT DIRECTLY TREAT PEOPLE.

RATHER THEY ACT AS MIDDLEMEN, MANAGING FUNDS THAT COME THROUGH THEIR FOUNDATION.

BILL RECEIVES PARADES, CELEBRATIONS, HONORS, PARTIES AND ADORATION WHEREVER HE GOES.

YOU SHOULDN'T HAVE!

WE LOVE ♥ BILL

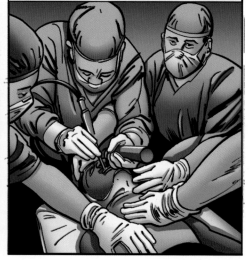

WHILE THE WORK OF TREATING THE ILL AND TERMINALLY ILL IS DONE BY "CARE PARTNERS" LIKE DOCTORS WITHOUT BORDERS, THE RED CROSS AND SAMARITAN'S PURSE.

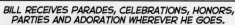

AND IN ANY THIRD WORLD HELL WHERE BILL SHOWS HIS FACE--

--AN ENTOURAGE OF INTERNATIONAL BUSINESSMEN TAG ALONG.

FRANK GIUSTRA

IT'S VERY NICE HERE THIS TIME OF YEAR.

THESE VISITS ALSO BENEFIT THE STRONGMEN AND DESPOTS WHO HOST BILL AND HIS SPECIAL FRIENDS.

LIKE PAUL KAGAME, PRESIDENT OF RWANDA.

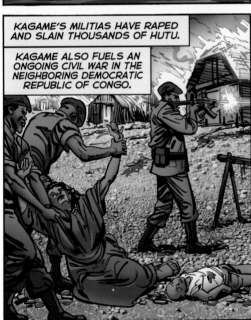

KAGAME'S MILITIAS HAVE RAPED AND SLAIN THOUSANDS OF HUTU.

KAGAME ALSO FUELS AN ONGOING CIVIL WAR IN THE NEIGHBORING DEMOCRATIC REPUBLIC OF CONGO.

HIS INVOLVEMENT WITH THE CLINTON FOUNDATION OFFERS HIM AND HIS REGIME AN INVALUABLE LEGITIMACY.

STOP ME IF YOU'VE HEARD THIS.

A TUTSI, A PYGMY AND A MISSIONARY WALK INTO A BAR...

HE IS QUICK TO PUBLICIZE HIS APPEARANCES WITH BILL.

PARTNERING WITH A FAMOUS EX-PRESIDENT OF THE UNITED STATES PROVIDES KAGAME COVER.

COVER THAT HE NEEDS TO BLUNT WORLD CRITICISM OF HIS PRESIDENCY'S HUMAN RIGHTS RECORD.

THE CLINTONS POINT OUT THAT NONE OF THE FAMILY TAKE A SALARY FROM THE FOUNDATION.

BUT, IN POST-PRESIDENTIAL YEARS, BILL RECEIVED SPEAKING FEES IN THE LOW-TO-MID SIX FIGURES.

BLAH BLAH BLAH WORLD ECONOMIC FORCES BLAH BLAH MICRO-LOANS BLAH

OVER THE YEARS HIS SPEECHES TURNED FROM HIS WORLD VIEW AND EXPERIENCES TO TALKING ABOUT THE WORK OF THE FOUNDATION.

CHING

CHING CHING

KA-CHING

A BOOK ABOUT HIS CHARITY EFFORTS EARNED HIM ANOTHER 6.5 MILLION IN ROYALTIES.

BILL CLINTON

GIVING

HOW EACH OF US CAN CHANGE THE WORLD

BLURRING THEIR CHARITABLE, POLITICAL, AND FINANCIAL INTERESTS HAS SERVED THE CLINTONS WELL.

WHEN HILLARY TAKES OVER STATE THE PRACTICE REACHES A WHOLE NEW LEVEL.

HAITI

HOW ARE WE SUPPOSED TO *FIND* THIS PLACE?

WITHOUT ROAD SIGNS? BY GUESS AND BY GOSH, I GUESS.

2013.

I *SWEAR* WE'VE BEEN PAST THIS PLACE THREE TIMES.

WE COULD CALL THE *CENTER* AND ASK FOR DIRECTIONS.

WE'VE *DONE* THAT. I THINK *THEY'RE* LOST TOO.

I'M GONNA ASK *THIS* GUY.

IS THAT A GOOD IDEA?

EXCUSE ME.

OUI?

WE'RE LOOKING FOR RUE BRUNACHE.

IS THAT AN IPAD?

UM... NO. IT'S A GALAXY.

THE CLINTON BLUR 2

HILLARY CLINTON PUSHED RUSSIAN OFFICIALS TO SIGN A 3.7 BILLION PURCHASE FOR JETS FROM BOEING.

BOEING WOULD THEN GIFT THE CLINTON FOUNDATION $900,000 AS WELL AS PAYING BILL A QUARTER MILLION FOR ONE SPEECH.

IT WAS PART OF WHAT HILLARY CALLED "COMMERCIAL DIPLOMACY" OR "ECONOMIC STATECRAFT."

THE IDEA WAS SIMPLE: SHE WOULD USE HER LEVERAGE AS HEAD OF STATE TO HELP AMERICAN COMPANIES BE MORE COMPETITIVE OVERSEAS.

BUT IN PRACTICE IT WOULD PROVE DIFFICULT TO DISTINGUISH THE PERSONAL AND POLITICAL ASPECTS OF THIS KIND OF ACTIVITY.

MILLENNIUM CHALLENGE CORPORATION (MCC) FOR EXAMPLE, A QUASI-FEDERAL AGENCY...

...WAS CHAIRED BY THE SECRETARY OF STATE.

BUT MCC INITIATIVES TENDED TO FAVOR POLITICALLY CONNECTED FIRMS.

SYMBION POWER, FOR EXAMPLE, WITH LONGTIME CLINTON FRIEND AND ALLY, JOE WILSON ON ITS BOARD, WAS FUNDED BY MCC.

HAVE YOU MET MY SECRET AGENT WIFE?

OR HECTATE ENERGY WHOSE FOUNDER, DAVID WILHELM, HAS NO BACKGROUND IN ENERGY GENERATION.

BUT HE **WAS** MANAGER OF BILL CLINTON'S 1992 PRESIDENTIAL CAMPAIGN.

SHORTLY AFTER HER CONFIRMATION AS SECRETARY OF STATE, HILLARY CREATED THE OFFICE OF GLOBAL PARTNERSHIPS.

OFFICE OF GLOBAL PARTNERSHIPS

A BRAND NEW INFRASTRUCTURE THAT HIRED MANY CLINTONISTAS TO FILL ITS POSITIONS.

THE **OGP** WOULD BE RUN BY KRIS BALDERSON, SOMEONE WITHOUT CORPORATE, DIPLOMATIC, OR OVERSEAS EXPERIENCE OF ANY KIND.

HIS MOST FAMOUS ROLE IN THE CLINTON WORLD WAS MAINTAINING BILL AND HILLARY'S ENEMIES LIST.

AND YOU WERE BAD! OO! VERY BAD!

OVERALL, HILLARY INCREASED STATE'S EMPLOYMENT ROLES BY 17% AND EMPLOYMENT AT USAID BY 30%.

HILLARY MADE EXTENSIVE USE OF THE SPECIAL GOVERNMENT EMPLOYEES RULE.

THIS SPECIAL CATEGORY WAS DESIGNED TO ENSURE THAT EXPERTS LIKE SCIENTISTS AND ENGINEERS COULD BE TAPPED FOR THEIR EXPERTISE.

UNDER HILLARY, THE SGE RULE BECAME A LOOPHOLE TO HIRE WHOM SHE WANTED WITHOUT OVERSIGHT OR APPROVAL.

LIKE HUMA ABEDIN WHO SERVED AS HILLARY'S DEPUTY CHIEF OF STAFF.

WHILE SIMULTANEOUSLY ON THE PAYROLL OF THE CLINTON FOUNDATION.

AS WELL AS **TENEO**, A CONSULTING FIRM STARTED IN 2009 BY DOUG BAND, A FRIEND OF BILL'S.

PAYDAY!

MANY MORE POSITIONS WERE NEWLY CREATED, AND FILLED BY FORMER MEMBERS OF EITHER HILLARY'S SENATE STAFF, OR BILL'S WHITE HOUSE STAFF.

THE HIGHEST PAYING, MOST INFLUENTIAL POSITIONS WENT TO EITHER CLOSE CLINTON ASSOCIATES OR FOUNDATION CONTRIBUTORS.

MILLS

SIDNEY BLUMENTHAL

ANN GAVAGHAN

CAITLIN KLEVORICK

ELIZABETH

ANOTHER TOOL TO CREATE PAYROLL OPPORTUNITIES FOR FRIENDS AND ALLIES IS THE **S**-CLASS DESIGNATION.

S-CLASS POSITIONS ARE UNDER THE DIRECT FINANCIAL CONTROL OF THE SECRETARY OF STATE AND NO ONE ELSE.

HILLARY ALSO DRAMATICALLY REDUCED THE INDEPENDENCE OF USAID.

SHE POPULATED THE AGENCY WITH LOYALISTS WHO HAD LITTLE OR NO RELEVANT EXPERIENCE.

MINE!

BY APPOINTING SO MANY SPECIAL STATUS EMPLOYEES, HILLARY BLURRED THE LINES BETWEEN AMERICAN DIPLOMATIC RELATIONS--

--AND THE INTERESTS OF THE CLINTONS AND THEIR FRIENDS.

CONSIDER *LAUREATE EDUCATION,* WHICH BEGAN AS PART OF *SYLVAN LEARNING SYSTEMS.*

LOOK, MOM!

LAUREATE, FOUNDED IN BALTIMORE IN 1999, IS THE LARGEST FOR-PROFIT UNIVERSITY SYSTEM IN THE WORLD.

CHAIRMAN DOUGLAS BECKER OVERSEES A SPRAWLING NETWORK OF CAMPUSES IN SAUDI ARABIA, CHINA, CYPRUS, BRAZIL AND MANY OTHER COUNTRIES ACROSS THE DEVELOPING WORLD.

IN BRAZIL ALONE, THERE ARE 130,000 STUDENTS PAYING TUITION TO ATTEND TEN LAUREATE SCHOOLS ON FORTY DIFFERENT CAMPUSES.

LAUREATE RECRUITS STUDENTS THROUGH TELEMARKETING.

FROM CALL CENTERS ON THE CAMPUSES THEMSELVES AND STAFFED BY STUDENTS.

THE UNIVERSITY SYSTEM SPENDS MORE THAN 200 MILLION DOLLARS A YEAR ON ADVERTISING ALL OVER THE DEVELOPING WORLD.

快乐！快乐！正在学习对我来说！*

LAUREATE
INTERNATIONAL
UNIVERSITIES

*HAPPY! HAPPY! IS LEARNING FOR ME!

IN 2010, BILL CLINTON SIGNED AS HONORARY CHANCELLOR OF LAUREATE.

FOR THIS HONOR HE IS PAID MORE THAN $16 MILLION OVER FIVE YEARS BY LAUREATE.

IN ADDITION TO MILLIONS PAID FOR SPEECHES AT LAUREATE SCHOOLS ALL OVER THE WORLD--

--BILL'S FACE AND NAME APPEAR ON POSTERS, BANNERS AND ADVERTISING MATERIALS.

BLAH BLAH SUSTAINABLE BLAH BLAH EDUCATION OPPORTUNITIES BLAH BLAH

LAUREATE
INTERNATIONAL
UNIVERSITIES

BUT LAUREATE'S BUSINESS PRACTICES ARE ACTUALLY ILLEGAL IN COUNTRIES LIKE MEXICO, CHILE AND TURKEY.

FOR-PROFIT UNIVERSITIES ARE AGAINST THE LAW IN THOSE COUNTRIES.

GOTTA PAY TO PLAY, KIDS.

DOUGLAS BECKER WORKS AROUND THESE RESTRICTIONS BY GETTING HIRED TO SIT ON UNIVERSITY BOARDS IN THOSE PLACES WHERE HIS BUSINESS IS CONSIDERED A CRIME.

IN ADDITION, THOSE SCHOOLS HIRE LAUREATE FOR SERVICES LIKE COMPUTER ADVISORY AND ENGLISH COURSES.

THEY ALSO CHARGE FOR USE OF THE LAUREATE TRADEMARK.

Adakah anda ingin kent goreng dengan itu?

Do you want fries th that?

ACCORDING TO CHILE'S ECONOMIC CRIMES UNIT, LAUREATE'S SCHOOLS THERE TRANSFERRED MORE THAN 80 MILLION DOLLARS OUT OF THE COUNTRY BETWEEN 2011 AND 2013.

ANYTHING TO DECLARE, SENOR?

Customs and Immigration

ONLY HOW LOVELY YOUR COUNTRY IS THIS TIME OF YEAR. MI AMIGO.

IN ADDITION TO RUNNING LAUREATE, BECKER IS ALSO CHAIRMAN OF THE INTERNATIONAL YOUTH FOUNDATION (IYF).

international youth foundation

HE PROMOTED THE NON-PROFIT AT THE CLINTON GLOBAL INITIATIVE ANNUAL MEETING IN 2010.

WITH BILL'S HEARTY ENDORSEMENT.

I AM PLEASED THAT LAUREATE INTERNATIONAL UNIVERSITIES AND THE INTERNATIONAL YOUTH FOUNDATION HAVE PARTNERED ON THIS COMMITMENT TO EMPOWER YOUNG SOCIAL ENTREPRENEURS BLAH BLAH BLAH...

SHORTLY AFTER, HILLARY MADE LAUREATE PART OF HER STATE DEPARTMENT GLOBAL PARTNERSHIP.

OO... LET'S PUT A PRETTY PINK ONE HERE.

IYF RECEIVED FUNDS FROM THE STATE DEPARTMENT THROUGH USAID IN ADDITION TO OTHER GOVERNMENT GRANTS.

23 MILLION IN 2010.
21 MILLION IN 2011.
23 MILLION IN 2012.

IN 2013, JUST BEFORE HILLARY LEFT HER POST AT STATE, THE INTERNATIONAL FINANCE CORPORATION MADE A 150 MILLION DOLLAR INVESTMENT IN LAUREATE.

AND ONE LAST THING, JIMMY...

THE IFC IS PART OF THE WORLD BANK.

THE HEAD OF WHICH AT THE TIME WAS JIM KIM.

THAT'S "BECKER." WITH A "B."

KIM IS A CLINTON FRIEND AS WELL AS COFOUNDER OF PARTNERS IN HEALTH, A PARTNER OF THE CLINTON FOUNDATION.

UH!

WOULD YOU LIKE A MULLIGAN, MR. PRESIDENT?

ISN'T IT TROUBLING THAT BILL WAS BEING PAID BY A PRIVATE CORPORATION THAT WAS ALSO BENEFITING FROM STATE DEPARTMENT ACTIONS?

ISN'T IT TROUBLING THAT AN AFFILIATE OF THIS CORPORATION WAS RECEIVING TENS OF MILLIONS OF TAXPAYER DOLLARS?

ISN'T IT TROUBLING THAT THIS CONFLICT OF INTEREST WAS NOT DISCLOSED?

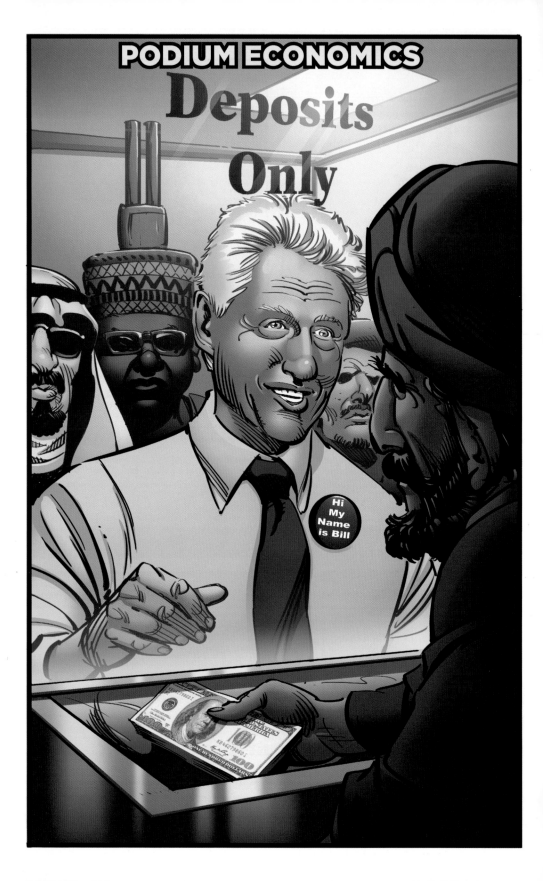

SPEECHES AT POPULAR PRICES

THAT WAS A TEN Y'ALL GAVE ME?

MOST EX-PRESIDENTS SEE THE DEMAND FOR THEIR SPEECHES DECLINE AS THEY MOVE FARTHER FROM THEIR TIME IN OFFICE.

RONALD REAGAN FAMOUSLY GAVE TWO SPEECHES IN TOKYO FOR TWO MILLION DOLLARS.

DOMO ARIGATO.

WELL, DOMO TO YOU TOO.

GEORGE H. W. BUSH JOINED CORPORATE BOARDS FOR INVESTMENT FIRMS AND OTHER INTERESTS.

WHAT EXACTLY IS IT THAT WE DO HERE?

BUT NO FORMER PRESIDENT COMES CLOSE TO BILL CLINTON'S EARNING POWER.

AND HERE WE SEE AN EARNING SPIKE AS HILLARY WINS THE SENATE SEAT.

AND THAT SPIKE THERE?

WHEN SHE WAS APPOINTED SECRETARY OF STATE. WE CALL THAT "THE JACKPOT."

AN EXAMPLE OF THE CORRELATION BETWEEN BILL'S SPEAKING FEES AND HILLARY'S POLITICAL INFLUENCE IS PROVIDED BY THE KEYSTONE XL PIPELINE.

BEGINNING IN 2008, TRANSCANADA CORPORATION SOUGHT US GOVERNMENT APPROVAL FOR AN ENVIRONMENTALLY-CONTROVERSIAL EIGHT BILLION DOLLAR PIPELINE.

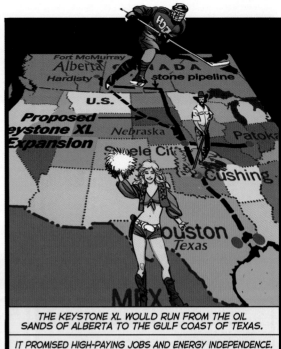

THE KEYSTONE XL WOULD RUN FROM THE OIL SANDS OF ALBERTA TO THE GULF COAST OF TEXAS.

IT PROMISED HIGH-PAYING JOBS AND ENERGY INDEPENDENCE.

TD BANK, A CANADIAN FINANCIAL INSTITUTION, HELD 1.6 BILLION IN SHARES OF THE PIPELINE.

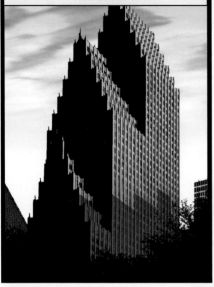

BANKER

THEY WERE ALSO ON THE HOOK FOR A FURTHER 993 MILLION IN LOANS.

IN NOVEMBER 2008, PRESIDENT-ELECT OBAMA ANNOUNCED HILLARY AS HIS NOMINEE TO HEAD THE STATE DEPARTMENT.

FOUR DAYS LATER, TD PAID BILL FOR WHAT WOULD BE THE FIRST OF TEN SPEECHES.

HELLO CANADA!

AFTER HILLARY'S CONFIRMATION, BILL RETURNED FOR THREE MORE SPEECHES AND ANOTHER $525,000.

BLAH BLAH... TIM HORTON'S DO-NUTS... BLAH BLAH... PEACEFUL BORDER...

IN ADDITION TO TD THROWING MILLIONS AT BILL, TRANS-CANADA HIRED CLINTON ASSOCIATES AS LOBBYISTS AND CONSULTANTS.

ENVIRONMENTAL IMPACT STUDIES WERE DONE BY COMPANIES WITH TIES TO TRANSCANADA.

YOU WILL LOBBY AND LOBBY IT'S YOUR JOB AND YOUR HOBBY YOU'LL DO WHAT I SAY FOR A FAT PAYDAY AND OPEN AN OFFICE ON AVENUE K.

LISTEN UP, *BOYEEEEEE!* JUST LISTEN TO ME. WE'LL BUILD A PIPELINE FROM HERE TO THE SEA!

CLOSE TIES BETWEEN THE CANADIAN COMPANIES AND THE US STATE DEPARTMENT DID NOT ESCAPE THE NOTICE OF ENVIRONMENTAL GROUPS.

DAMON MOGLEN, DIRECTOR FOR FRIENDS OF THE EARTH SAID:

"I THINK WE'VE GONE WAY BEYOND BIAS.

WE NOW SEE THAT THE STATE DEPARTMENT HAS BEEN COMPLICIT IN THIS ENTIRE AFFAIR."

HILLARY WOULD FIND HERSELF TORN BETWEEN TWO RELIABLE DEMOCRAT CONSTITUENCIES.

IT WILL MEAN JOBS!

IT WILL MEAN THE POISONING OF NATURE!

BOTH OF YOU MAKE EXCELLENT ARGUMENTS.

HILLARY'S POSITION REMAINED MADDENINGLY EVASIVE.

WE'RE EITHER GOING TO BE DEPENDENT ON DIRTY OIL FROM THE PERSIAN GULF OR DIRTY OIL FROM CANADA.

WHILE PRESIDENT OBAMA STALLED MAKING ANY KIND OF DECISION.

AMERICA SHOULD **EMBRACE** THE PIPELINE.

BILL ANNOUNCED HIS FIRM SUPPORT AT (OF ALL PLACES) A DEPARTMENT OF ENERGY CONFERENCE FOR CLEAN TECHNOLOGY.

WHEN ASKED ABOUT HER HUSBAND'S STRONG POSITION, HILLARY SAID:

HE'S A VERY SMART MAN.

TEE HEE.

BARACK OBAMA DECIDED TO PUT ANY DECISION OFF UNTIL AFTER THE 2012 PRESIDENTIAL ELECTION.

THIS EFFECTIVELY KILLED THE PROJECT.

ESPECIALLY AS, WITH OBAMA'S RE-ELECTION, HILLARY WOULD LEAVE THE STATE DEPARTMENT.

YOU CALL THAT A BOOK ADVANCE?

IN THE END THE KEYSTONE PIPELINE DID NOT GO FORWARD.

BUT THE CLINTONS GOT PAID REGARDLESS.

THE SWEDISH TELECOM GIANT ERICSSON ROUTINELY DOES BUSINESS IN NATIONS SUCH AS SYRIA AND SUDAN WHO SPONSOR TERRORISM.

IN IRAN, ERICSSON'S FOOTPRINT WAS BROAD AS A LAND-BASED AND MOBILE TELECOMMUNICATIONS PROVIDER.

لى ح ي ي ص الة ع ح ي أو ال لى...ع ۋ

...SO THEN MUKTAR SAID...

IN 2011, THE STATE DEPARTMENT BEGAN COMPILING A LIST OF WHICH GOODS AND SERVICES MIGHT BE COVERED IN EXPANDED SANCTIONS ON IRAN.

ERICSSON HAD NEVER SPONSORED A CLINTON SPEECH.

BUT THEY DECIDED THAT THE TIME WAS RIGHT TO PAY BILL $750,000 FOR A SINGLE SPEECH.

BLAH BLAH BLAH AFFORDABLE TELEPHONE SERVICE BLAH BLAH

THE HIGHEST FEE HE'D EVER RECEIVED.

ONE WEEK AFTER THE SPEECH, THE STATE DEPARTMENT UNVEILED ITS NEW SANCTIONS LIST FOR IRAN.

TELECOM WAS NOT ON THAT LIST.

TENSIONS BETWEEN THE US AND CHINA HAVE BEEN ON THE RISE IN RECENT YEARS.

INTO THESE STRAINED RELATIONS COMES BILL CLINTON, ACCEPTING LARGE FEES TO MAKE SPEECHES IN CHINA--

SPONSORED EITHER BY INFLUENTIAL GOVERNMENT MINISTERS OR DIRECTLY FROM AGENCIES OF THE PEOPLE'S REPUBLIC.

BUT WHAT ARE THE **ETHICS** OF SUCH TRANSACTIONS?

THE STATE DEPARTMENT'S ETHICS OFFICE IS CLEAR ON THIS.

CONTRIBUTIONS FROM THE PRC ARE NOT ALLOWED.

Aristotle Socrates Billius

BILL SUBMITTED HIS SPEECH PROPOSALS TO THE STATE DEPARTMENT FOR APPROVAL--

--BUT THE EMPHASIS FOR ETHICS OFFICERS WAS SPEED OVER DILIGENCE.

HAROLD KOH, STATE'S LEGAL ADVISOR, RAN THE ETHICS OFFICE.

KOH WAS A FORMER CLINTON ADMINISTRATION APPOINTEE.

ALL PROPOSALS TO THE ETHICS OFFICE WERE CC'ED TO CHERYL MILLS, LONGTIME CLINTON FRIEND.

MILLS REPORTED DIRECTLY TO HILLARY.

HAITI

ESKIZE M ', MSYE.

I AM LOOKING FOR WORK.

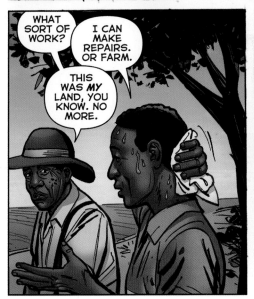

WHAT SORT OF WORK?

I CAN MAKE REPAIRS. OR FARM.

THIS WAS *MY* LAND, YOU KNOW. NO MORE.

I PLANTED THAT TREE BEFORE MY CHILDREN WERE BORN.

THEY HAVE LEFT ME. NOW THE TREE IS GONE AS WELL.

WARLORD ECONOMICS

ON ANY LIST OF THE "THE WORST PLACES ON EARTH", THE DEMOCRATIC REPUBLIC OF CONGO WOULD RANK NEAR THE TOP.

YEARS OF CIVIL WAR AND CORRUPT DICTATORS.

AND CHILDREN DRAFTED AS SOLDIERS.

AND REFUGEES WANDERING HOMELESS AND HUNGRY.

AND THE DEAD, THE MAIMED AND THE RAPED.

2009.

SECRETARY OF STATE HILLARY CLINTON LANDED IN KINSHASHA, **DRC.**

SHE WAS HOSTED BY **NBA** STAR DIKEMBE MUTOMBO, WHO WAS BORN IN THE CONGO.

DESPITE THE CONGO'S REPUTATION AS A HOUSE OF HORRORS, THE VISIT APPEARED TO BE A GOODWILL TOUR.

HILLARY SPOKE TO COLLEGE STUDENTS.

WE KNOW THAT THE PROMISE OF THE DRC IS LIMITLESS.

AS WELL AS MEETING WITH JOSEPH KABILA, THE STRONGMAN PRESIDENT OF THE DRC.

I AM PARTICULARLY CONCERNED ABOUT THE EXPLOITATION OF NATURAL RESOURCES.

BUT WHERE WAS THE HILLARY CLINTON WHO SERVED AS US SENATOR?

THESE *ATROCITIES,* THESE MASS RAPES AND MASS MURDERS, MUST *STOP!*

2006.

SHE CO-SPONSORED THE **DEMOCRATIC REPUBLIC OF CONGO RELIEF, SECURITY, AND DEMOCRACY PROMOTION ACT** WITH THEN-SENATOR BARACK OBAMA.

I CARE.

I CARE MORE.

PRESIDENT BUSH SIGNED THE BILL INTO LAW.

AND THE LAW HAD REAL TEETH TO PUNISH COMPANIES DOING BUSINESS WITH THE CORRUPT CONGOLESE REGIME.

BUT, AS SECRETARY OF STATE, HILLARY DID **NOT** USE THE PROVISIONS OF THE LAW TO SANCTION EITHER THE VILE KABILA OR HIS WESTERN BUSINESS PARTNERS.

IN 2011, THE DRC HELD ELECTIONS THAT WERE WIDELY CONDEMNED.

EVEN WHEN THE CONSTITUTION WAS CHANGED IN FAVOR OF PRESIDENT KABILA, THE US STATE DEPARTMENT CALLED IT "AN INTERNAL AFFAIR."

THE ARMY OF NEIGHBORING RWANDA ENTERED THE CONGO IN SUPPORT OF KABILA'S MILITIA.

THE RESULT WAS DEATHS IN THE HUNDREDS OF THOUSANDS.

HILLARY'S STATE DEPARTMENT QUIETLY ASKED RWANDA TO WITHDRAW.

YOU HAVE TO SEE THIS SELFIE SIDNEY SENT ME!

HILLARY ANNOUNCED HER FIRST BID FOR THE WHITE HOUSE.

I'M IN.

AND I'M IN TO WIN.

INTRODUCING LUKAS LUNDIN, SWEDISH MINING BILLIONAIRE.

CLOSE FRIEND OF FRANK GIUSTRA.

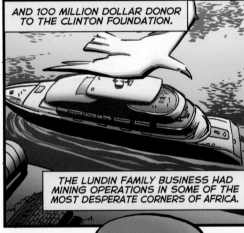

AND 100 MILLION DOLLAR DONOR TO THE CLINTON FOUNDATION.

THE LUNDIN FAMILY BUSINESS HAD MINING OPERATIONS IN SOME OF THE MOST DESPERATE CORNERS OF AFRICA.

THE SPRAWLING ENTERPRISE CUT DEALS WITH WARLORDS AND DICTATORS TO GAIN ACCESS TO VALUABLE MINERALS AND OIL.

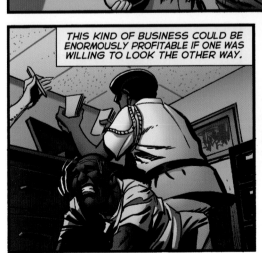

THIS KIND OF BUSINESS COULD BE ENORMOUSLY PROFITABLE IF ONE WAS WILLING TO LOOK THE OTHER WAY.

THE LUNDIN GROUP WAS UNDER INVESTIGATION BY THE INTERNATIONAL PROSECUTION CHAMBER IN STOCKHOLM.

FOR COMPLICITY IN WAR CRIMES AND CRIMES AGAINST HUMANITY.

LUKAS LUNDIN'S FATHER WAS ADOLPH LUNDIN, WHO BUILT A FORTUNE BY MINING IN APARTHEID SOUTH AFRICA.

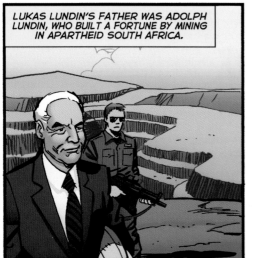

HIS OPERATIONS SPANNED THE CONTINENT, MINING AND DRILLING IN SINKHOLES OF CORRUPTION LIKE ETHIOPIA.

AND LAWLESS REGIONS LIKE SOMALIA.

BUT MOST LUCRATIVE OF ALL WERE HIS DEALS STRUCK WITH LAURENT KABILA.

HE FINANCED KABILA'S CONGOLESE COUP WITH HUNDREDS OF MILLIONS OF DOLLARS IN EXCHANGE FOR UNLIMITED MINERAL RIGHTS.

IN ADOLPH'S OWN WORDS:

THERE ARE MOMENTS IN THE HISTORY OF MINING WHEN YOU CAN MAKE DEALS LIKE THIS UNDER EXCELLENT TERMS.

OVER THE NEXT DECADES, THE LUNDIN GROUP'S PROFITS IN THE CONGO WERE STAGGERING.

IT WAS IN THEIR INTEREST THAT CONDITIONS REMAIN STATUS QUO.

THAT STATUS QUO WAS PRESERVED BY HILLARY CLINTON'S DISAPPOINTING FAILURE--

--TO IMPLEMENT THE LAW THAT SHE HAS ADVOCATED FOR ONLY A FEW YEARS EARLIER.

HILLARY'S HOST FOR HER VISIT TO THE CONGO WAS DIKEMBE MUTOMBO, FORMER STAR OF THE DENVER NUGGETS.

BUT IT WAS FAR **MORE** THAN NUGGETS AT THE CENTER OF A DEAL MUTOMBO ENTERED INTO WITH KASE LAWAL, A HILLARY FOR PRESIDENT CAMPAIGN BUNDLER.

THE PAIR CONSPIRED TO EXPORT 4.5 TONS OF GOLD FROM THE CONGO.

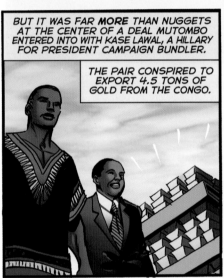

THE MAN WHO FACILITATED THE DEAL WAS BOSCO NTAGANDA, A NOTORIOUS WAR CRIMINAL AND HUMAN RIGHTS VIOLATOR SANCTIONED BY INTERNATIONAL AGENCIES INCLUDING OUR OWN TREASURY DEPARTMENT.

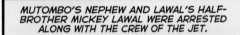

ANY US CITIZEN DOING BUSINESS WITH HIM WAS RISKING UP TO TWENTY YEARS IMPRISONMENT.

THE DEAL WAS SET BACK WHEN THE JET CARRYING THE GOLD WAS CONFISCATED BY GOVERNMENT AUTHORITIES IN GOMA.

MUTOMBO'S NEPHEW AND LAWAL'S HALF-BROTHER MICKEY LAWAL WERE ARRESTED ALONG WITH THE CREW OF THE JET.

MUTOMBO PLACED A PHONE CALL TO THE STATE DEPARTMENT.

THEY WERE RELEASED AFTER INTERVENTION FROM THE US STATE DEPARTMENT.

NO ONE INVOLVED HAS FACED CRIMINAL CHARGES.

EVERYTHING HAS A PRICE IN AFRICA.

EVEN JUSTICE.

REMEMBER JOE WILSON?

SO, THEN MY WIFE, THE *SECRET AGENT*, SAYS--I *DID* TELL YOU MY WIFE WAS A *SPY*, RIGHT?

IN ADDITION TO BEING A CLINTON FRIEND AND HILLARY CAMPAIGN ORGANIZER--

--WILSON IS ALSO A BIG PLAYER IN AFRICA.

I MEAN, MY WIFE WAS LIKE SOME KIND OF JAMES BOND.

CHAMES BOMB?

HIS FORMER POSITION IN THE CLINTON STATE DEPARTMENT GAVE HIM AN ENTRÉE TO THE CONTINENT.

SHE'S LIKE JASON BOURNE.

MATT HELM?

SECRET SQUIRREL?

IT WAS WILSON WHO BROUGHT BILL TO AFRICA FOR THE FIRST TIME.

THE TRIP SUPPOSEDLY RAISED CLINTON'S CONSCIOUSNESS CONCERNING THE CONTINENT.

THERE'S REALLY MONEY HERE, JOE?

WILSON WAS VICE-CHAIRMAN OF JARCH CAPITAL.

A NEW YORK BASED HOLDING COMPANY.

JARCH

JARCH CUT DEALS FOR RIGHTS TO OIL, URANIUM AND GOLD IN COUNTRIES WHERE IT EXPECTED "SOVEREIGNTY CHANGES."

OIL

THAT'S A NICE WAY OF SAYING COUNTRIES THAT ARE AT WAR.

AS JARCH FOUNDER PHILIPPE HEILBERG WAS FOND OF SAYING:

YOU HAVE TO GO TO THE GUNS. THIS IS AFRICA.

WILSON WAS AN EXPERT IN THIS AREA. AS A FORMER AMBASSADOR TO SEVERAL AFRICAN NATIONS, HE UNDERSTOOD HOW TO DEAL WITH WARLORDS, PETTY TYRANTS AND DICTATORS.

SHORTLY AFTER HILLARY'S APPOINTMENT AS SECRETARY OF STATE, JARCH ACQUIRED A FIFTY YEAR LEASE TO A SECTION OF SUDAN THE SIZE OF VERMONT.

THE DEAL HAD A "DECIDEDLY 19TH CENTURY FLAVOR TO IT."*

*FINANCIAL TIMES 1-10-2009

WITH CIVIL WAR RAGING, THE US GOVERNMENT PUT RESTRICTIONS ON AMERICAN COMPANIES DOING BUSINESS THERE.

JARCH SET UP A FOREIGN-BASED SUBSIDIARY AND KEPT ON AS BEFORE.

JARCH ENTERED INTO DEALS OR ACTUALLY GAVE JOBS TO QUESTIONABLE FIGURES LIKE GENERAL PAULINO MATIP NHIAL.

DEPUTY COMMANDER IN CHIEF OF THE SUDANESE LIBERATION ARMY.

GENERAL PAULINO MATIP NHIAL

OR GENERAL GABRIEL TANGINYA, ACCUSED OF INSTIGATING VIOLENCE AGAINST CIVILIANS IN SOUTHERN SUDAN.

GENERAL GABRIEL TANGINYA

AND RIEK MACHAR, VICE-PRESIDENT OF SOUTH SUDAN AND CONTRIBUTOR TO THE INFAMOUS BOR MASSACRE.

FOR WHICH HE APOLOGIZED.

I'M SORRY. I REALLY AM.

PETER GADET WAS GIVEN A POSITION ON A JARCH ADVISORY BOARD, THEN REMOVED WHEN FACING INTERNATIONAL SANCTIONS FOR A LIST OF ATROCITIES.

GENERAL PETER GADET

NIGERIA IS ONE OF THE MOST CORRUPT NATIONS ON EARTH.

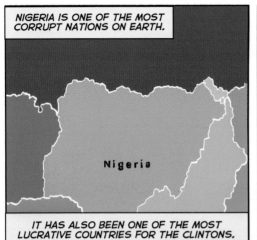

Nigeria

IT HAS ALSO BEEN ONE OF THE MOST LUCRATIVE COUNTRIES FOR THE CLINTONS.

BILL CLINTON HAD NEVER GIVEN A SPEECH IN NIGERIA.

BLAH BLAH AIDS BLAH BLAH INTERNATIONAL COMMUNITY BLAH BLAH

UNTIL HIS WIFE BECAME SECRETARY OF STATE.

HE WAS PAID $700,000 EACH FOR TWO SPEECHES.

UNDERWRITTEN BY MEDIA MOGUL NDUKA OBAIGBENA.

HAKUNA MATATA!

AT OBAIGBENA'S REQUEST, BILL PARTICIPATED IN AN AWARDS CEREMONY WHERE HE HANDED OUT CHECKS TO SCHOOL TEACHERS AS REWARDS FOR THEIR WORK.

ALL THE CHECKS BOUNCED.

RETURNED Insufficient Funds

OBAIGBENA HAD A CLOSE RELATIONSHIP WITH GOODLUCK JONATHAN, DICTATOR OF NIGERIA.

GOODLUCK JONATHAN

JONATHAN IS NOTORIOUSLY PROFLIGATE WITH NIGERIA'S TREASURY.

SPENDING LAVISHLY TO IMPORT JAY-Z AND BEYONCE FOR A CONCERT.

TO PAY FOR THE CONCERT, JONATHAN TRANSFERRED ONE MILLION DOLLARS TO OBAIGBENA.

FROM NIGERIA'S POVERTY ALLEVIATION FUND.

ANOTHER AFRICAN PLAYER WITH STRONG TIES TO THE CLINTONS IS GILBERT CHAGOURY, A LEBANESE WITH DUAL CITIZENSHIP IN THE UNITED KINGDOM.

GILBERT CHAGOURY

CHAGOURY'S PARTNER IN HIS NIGERIAN VENTURES WAS MARC RICH.

THE FRAUDSTER THAT BILL CLINTON FAMOUSLY PARDONED.

MARC RICH

CHAGOURY'S LARGEST ROLE IN NIGERIAN CORRUPTION WAS MONEY LAUNDERING.

HE ILLEGALLY EXPORTED FOUR BILLION DOLLARS FROM THE COUNTRY INTO SWITZERLAND.

HE WAS CONVICTED IN A GENEVA COURT OF LAUNDERING AND AIDING A CRIMINAL ORGANIZATION.

HE PAID 300 MILLION IN EXCHANGE FOR IMMUNITY.

FOR SOME REASON, CHAGOURY WAS MADE AN ENVOY FOR UNESCO BY THE TINY ISLAND STATE OF ST. LUCIA.

THE POSITION GAVE HIM DIPLOMATIC IMMUNITY FROM FURTHER PROSECUTION IN EUROPE.

DESPITE ALLEGATIONS, CONVICTIONS AND SUSPECT ASSOCIATIONS, CHAGOURY'S RELATIONSHIP WITH THE CLINTONS BLOSSOMED.

HE PLEDGED A WHOPPING ONE **BILLION** DOLLARS TO THE CLINTON FOUNDATION.

BILL WAS PRESENT WHEN CHAGOURY WAS AWARDED A PRIDE OF HERITAGE PRIZE FROM THE LEBANESE COMMUNITY.

IN 2010, CHAGOURY WAS INDICTED IN A SIX BILLION DOLLAR BRIBERY DEAL WITH HALLIBURTON.

CHAGOURY WALKED BUT HALLIBURTON PAID 35 MILLION TO THE FEDERAL GOVERNMENT.

BUT CHAGOURY IS JUST ONE OF A DUBIOUS CAST OF CHARACTERS OPERATING IN A COUNTRY ONCE DESCRIBED AS "THE GLOBAL CAPITAL OF CORRUPTION."

WHO DESCRIBED NIGERIA THAT WAY?

NO LESS AN EXPERT THAN MARC RICH.

COLOMBIA WAS THE FOURTH LARGEST RECIPIENT OF MILITARY AND FOREIGN AID FROM THE UNITED STATES.

THE COUNTRY WAS COMING OUT OF MORE THAN A DECADE OF BATTLING NARCOTERRORISM.

I GIVE YOU THE BEST DEAL, SENOR.

I DUNNO. WHAT'D'YA THINK, EILEEN?

PRESIDENT ALVARO URIBE WAS ANXIOUS TO HAVE A MORE TRADITIONAL TRADING PARTNER STATUS WITH THE USA.

URIBE REACHED OUT TO BILL CLINTON THROUGH SPEAKING ENGAGEMENTS AND AWARDS.

THE COLOMBIA IS PASSION IS AWARD FOR YOU.

I'LL TREASURE IT ALWAYS.

BUT CANDIDATE HILLARY WAS VEHEMENTLY OPPOSED TO ANY KIND OF TRADE AGREEMENT.

I WILL DO *EVERYTHING* I CAN TO URGE CONGRESS TO REJECT THE COLOMBIA FREE TRADE AGREEMENT.

LATER, SECRETARY OF STATE CLINTON WAS ALL FOR IT AFTER VISITING THE COUNTRY.

AND I RETURN VERY INVIGORATED... TO BEGIN A VERY INTENSIVE EFFORT TO TRY TO OBTAIN THE VOTES TO GET THE FREE TRADE AGREEMENT FINALLY RATIFIED.

HILLARY DEFENDED HER CHANGE OF HEART BY SAYING THAT THE HUMAN RIGHTS AND LABOR SITUATION HAD IMPROVED IN COLOMBIA--

EXCEPT THAT A REPORT FROM HER OWN STATE DEPARTMENT CITED RISING MURDERS AMONG UNION MEMBERS.

CLOSING RANKS WITH THEIR UNION BROTHERS, THE AFL-CIO PROCLAIMED COLOMBIA "THE MOST DANGEROUS PLACE IN THE WORLD FOR UNION MEMBERS."

SO WHAT **HAPPENED** ON THAT TRIP TO COLOMBIA THAT CHANGED HILLARY'S MIND?

WELL, THE **DAY** BEFORE SHE ARRIVED, BILL AND FRANK GIUSTRA LANDED IN BOGOTA.

IN HER MEMOIR SHE CALLED THIS SERENDIPITY:

A HAPPY **COINCIDENCE** IN OUR HECTIC SCHEDULES.

BILL MET WITH PRESIDENT URIBE FOR BREAKFAST.

AND, A FEW HOURS LATER, HILLARY MET WITH HIM FOR LUNCH.

FIRST, LET ME UNDER-SCORE PRESIDENT OBAMA'S AND MY COMMITMENT TO THE FREE TRADE AGREEMENT.

THIS WAS A DIRECT REVERSAL OF HILLARY--AND OBAMA'S--POSITION ONLY A YEAR BEFORE.

I WANT TO CUT AID TO COLOMBIA.

I WANT TO CUT IT MORE.

NOT MORE THAN ME!

OH, WAY MORE!

WITHIN DAYS OF THE CLINTONS' BREAKFAST AND LUNCH WITH URIBE--

--THE GOVERNMENT GRANTED LOGGING RIGHTS TO PRIMA COLOMBIA PROPERTIES.

DAYS AFTER THAT THEY GRANTED OIL EXPLORATION RIGHTS TO PACIFIC RUBIALES.

AND WHAT DID THESE TWO CORPORATIONS HAVE IN COMMON?

I WAS LOOKING FOR ONE WITH MORE DIAMONDS.

CLINTON PAL, FRANK GIUSTRA HAD INTEREST IN BOTH FIRMS.

PACIFIC RUBIALES ALONE CONTRIBUTED OVER FOUR MILLION DOLLARS TO THE CLINTON FOUNDATION.

ANOTHER GIUSTRA INTEREST, PETROAMERICA, WENT FROM A PART-TIME OPERATION TO BIGTIME OIL FIRM WITHIN MONTHS.

CAN YOU TELL ME WHERE YOUR OFFICE IS?

THIS IS OUR OFFICE.

TAKE MY MONEY!

ME TOO!

ACCORDING TO LEAKED STATE DEPARTMENT MEMOS, THE U.S. TRADE DEVELOPMENT AGENCY AND THE EXPORT-IMPORT BANK WERE ANXIOUS TO DO BUSINESS.

THEY WOULD PROVIDE FINANCIAL BACKING GUARANTEED BY AMERICAN TAXPAYERS.

PATRICIA ARRIGADA

SILVANA GIAIMO

TDA REP PATRICIA ARRIGADA TRAVELLED TO COLOMBIA TO MEET WITH SILVANA GIAIMO, MINES AND ENERGY MINISTER.

OLE!

MANUEL OLIVERA

THEY WERE JOINED BY MANUEL OLIVERA, LOCAL DIRECTOR OF THE CLINTON FOUNDATION.

EVENTUALLY FRANK GIUSTRA WOULD HAVE OWNERSHIP OR INTEREST IN AGRICULTURE, OIL, PORTS, TRANSPORT, TIMBER, MINING AND POWER ACROSS COLOMBIA.

PICK A BUSINESS CARD, ANY CARD.

HIS WEB OF SHELL COMPANIES, FOREIGN ENTITIES, AND OFFSHORE AFFILIATES MAKE A CLEAR ASSESSMENT OF HOW MANY TAX PAYER DOLLARS WENT TO AID GIUSTRA IMPOSSIBLE.

JANUARY 13, 2010.

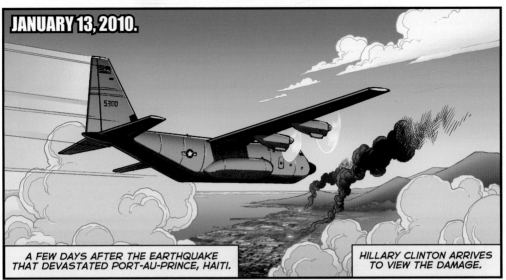

A FEW DAYS AFTER THE EARTHQUAKE THAT DEVASTATED PORT-AU-PRINCE, HAITI.

HILLARY CLINTON ARRIVES TO VIEW THE DAMAGE.

ALL FLIGHTS TO AND FROM THE STRICKEN ISLAND ARE HALTED FOR THREE HOURS FOR HER.

HILLARY ARRIVED WITH A SUPPLY OF MUSTARD, TOOTHPASTE AND CIGARETTES HER STAFF PURCHASED AT SUPERMARKETS THE NIGHT BEFORE.

BON JOU, TIMOUN MWEN AN ADVÈSITE!*

*GOOD DAY, MY CHILDREN OF ADVERSITY!

IN HIS ROLE AS SPECIAL ENVOY TO HAITI, BILL WAS ON THE GROUND SHORTLY AFTER.

IN EFFECT, HAITI'S NEW RULERS HAD ARRIVED.

WITHIN DAYS THE STATE DEPARTMENT CREATED A FUNNEL FOR THE RELIEF MONEY THAT WOULD FLOOD INTO THE COUNTRY.

THE INTERIM HAITI RECOVERY COMMISSION (IHRC) WAS BORN.

INTERIM HAITI RECOVERY COMMISSION

CHERYL MILLS, CLOSE FRIEND AND CONFIDANTE OF THE CLINTONS, WAS PUT IN CHARGE.

HER PRIORITY WAS THE RE-BUILDING OF PORT-AU-PRINCE AND THE HAITIAN ECONOMY.

CHERYL MILLS

HER **SUPPOSED** PRIORITY.

WOO!

FWOOOSSHHH!

BILL WAS APPOINTED CO-CHAIR OF THE IHRC.

HE PROMISED TO TRANSFORM HAITI.

FIVE YEARS, AND BILLIONS IN TAXPAYER AND PRIVATE DOLLARS LATER, HAITI IS MUCH THE SAME AS IT WAS AFTER THE QUAKE.

US AMBASSADOR TO HAITI KENNETH MERTEN GAVE HIS ASSESSMENT OF THE TRAGEDY IN HAITI IN A CABLE FROM PORT-AU-PRINCE TO THE STATE DEPARTMENT.

CHA-CHING!

MEMO
THE GOLD RUSH IS ON.

TO OVERSEE RECONSTRUCTION EFFORTS AND INVESTIGATE ALLEGATIONS OF CORRUPTION, A PERFORMANCE AND ANTI-CORRUPTION OFFICE WAS CALLED FOR.

IT WAS ELEVEN MONTHS BEFORE A SINGLE EMPLOYEE WAS HIRED.

IN THOSE KEY EARLY MONTHS, CONTRACTORS LIKE BERGERON RUSHED TO PARTICIPATE IN WHAT FOUNDER J.R. BERGERON CALLED "THE SUPER BOWL OF DISASTERS."

BERGERON

ANOTHER CONTRACTOR LOOKING FOR A PAYDAY IN HAITI WAS INNOVIDA, A FLORIDA-BASED COMPANY OWNED BY CLAUDIO OSORIO.

HE WAS A FUNDRAISER FOR HILLARY AND HEAVY CLINTON FOUNDATION CONTRIBUTOR.

OSORIO'S FRONT MAN IN HAITI WAS BILL CLINTON'S FAVORITE GENERAL, WESLEY CLARK.

HOO-AH!

CLARK

OSORIO'S COMPANY RECEIVED A TEN MILLION DOLLAR LOAN FROM THE U.S. GOVERNMENT TO BUILD 500 HOUSES IN HAITI.

INNOVIDA ACTUALLY HAD VERY LITTLE EXPERIENCE BUILDING HOMES.

EVEN SO, WESLEY CLARK MADE LOTS OF PROMISES FOR THE COMPANY.

IT CAN DO MORE FOR HOUSING IN HAITI, BETTER AND FASTER, THAN ANY OTHER TECHNOLOGY OUT THERE.

SADLY, NO HOUSES WERE EVER BUILT.

OSORIO WAS INDICTED AND CONVICTED OF FINANCIAL FRAUD.

HE IS CURRENTLY SERVING A TWELVE-YEAR SENTENCE.

IT'S HARD TO OVERSTATE THE POWER THE CLINTONS WIELDED IN THE DISBURSEMENT OF US TAXPAYER DOLLARS.

THE MEDIA REFERRED TO BILL AS "THE CEO OF A LEADERLESS NATION," "THE PRESIDENT OF HAITI," AND "VICEROY."

THE POWERBASE ONLY GREW WHEN GARRY CONILLE, FORMER CLINTON SPEECHWRITER, BECAME HAITI'S NEW PRIME MINISTER.

BLAH BLAH BLAH?

BLAH BLAH BLAH, SIR.

AS THE ECONOMIST SUCCINCTLY NOTED:

"THE STRANGE MULTI-DIMENSIONAL ROLE THAT MR. CLINTON PLAYS AS CO-CHAIR OF THE IHRC, SPECIAL UN ENVOY, FORMER US PRESIDENT, SPOUSE OF THE US SECRETARY OF STATE, AND HEAD OF HIS OWN FOUNDATION WHICH SUPPORTS PROJECTS ON THE COUNTRY, WILL CONTINUE TO LEAD TO CONFUSION ABOUT WHO HE ADVOCATES FOR AND TO WHOM HE ULTIMATELY ANSWERS."

IHRC MEMBERS AND EMPLOYEES ENSURED THAT BILL AND HILLARY GOT WHAT THEY WANTED WHEN IT CAME TO HAITI PROJECTS AND CONTRACTS.

MOSTLY, *IHRC* STAFFERS WERE LEFT OUT OF ADVISORY OR OVERSIGHT ACTIONS.

THE GOVERNMENT ACCOUNTING OFFICES OFFERED THEIR OPINION:

FUNDING FOR APPROVED PROJECTS IS UNEVEN ACROSS SECTORS AND IS NOT NECESSARILY ALIGNED WITH HAITIAN PRIORITIES.

WHEN HE WAS PRESIDENT, ONE OF BILL'S PET PROJECTS WAS BRINGING WIRELESS TELEPHONE TECHNOLOGY TO HAITI.

WOULDN'T IT BE *GREAT* IF THEY COULD BECOME THE *FIRST* WIRELESS NATION IN THE WORLD?

A SPECIAL DEAL WAS GRANTED TO FUSION COMMUNICATIONS.

SITTING ON THE BOARD OF FUSION WAS MACK McLARTY, BILL'S FORMER CHIEF OF STAFF.

THE BOARD WAS HEADED BY MARVIN ROSEN, THE DNC FINANCE COMMITTEE CHAIR DURING CLINTON'S FIRST TERM.

UNDER HIS TENURE THE NOTORIOUS FUND-RAISING COFFEES, RENTAL OF THE LINCOLN BEDROOM AND FOREIGN DONATIONS FROM CHINA OCCURRED.

FUSION'S SPECIAL ARRANGEMENT WITH THE HAITIAN GOVERNMENT-OWNED TELECOM COMPANY WAS SUPPOSED TO BE PUBLIC.

THE COMPANY WORKED HARD TO KEEP IT SECRET.

FUNDS FROM TAXPAYERS AND CHARITABLE FOUNDATIONS WERE POURED INTO BILL'S DREAM OF A WIRELESS HAITI.

THE BIG WINNER FROM THE HAITIAN DISASTER WAS THE IRISH FIRM **DIGICEL**, ANOTHER LARGE CLINTON DONOR.

DIGICEL IS OWNED BY IRISH BILLIONAIRE DENIS O'BRIEN.

O'BRIEN ARRANGED FOR BILL TO GIVE SPEECHES IN IRELAND AND WAS A MAJOR CONTRIBUTOR TO THE CLINTON FOUNDATION.

KISS THE BLARNEY STONE? THE BLARNEY STONE KISSED *ME!*

HAITIANS WERE GIVEN FREE PHONES AND ACCOUNTS IN TCHOTCHO MOBILE.*

* TCHOTCHO IS CREOLE FOR POCKET CHANGE.

BILL WAS PAID BY DIGICEL AND DIGICEL WAS PAID BY FUNDS COMING FROM, AMONG OTHER PLACES, THE **USAID** FOOD FOR PEACE PROGRAM.

IN ADDITION TO PAYING BILL EXORBITANT SPEAKING FEES, O'BRIEN DONATED AS MUCH AS FIVE MILLION TO THE CLINTON FOUNDATION.

BEGORRAH, Y'ALL.

AND WHILE THE **PHONES** WERE FREE, THE **SERVICE** WAS NOT.

HAITI QUICKLY BECAME DIGICEL'S MOST PROFITABLE MARKET.

ANOTHER BONANZA WAITED BENEATH THE HAITIAN SOIL.

AN ESTIMATED 20 BILLION DOLLARS IN GOLD LIES UNTAPPED THERE.

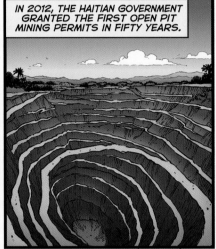

IN 2012, THE HAITIAN GOVERNMENT GRANTED THE FIRST OPEN PIT MINING PERMITS IN FIFTY YEARS.

ONE OF TWO RECIPIENTS OF A PERMIT WAS **VCS MINING**.

ONE SEAT ON THE BOARD OF **VCS** WOULD BE HELD BY HILLARY'S BROTHER TONY RODHAM--

--WHILE ANOTHER WAS HELD BY JEAN-MAX BELLERIVE, FORMER HAITIAN PRIME MINISTER AND CO-CHAIR OF THE **IHRC** ALONG WITH BILL.

IN A SWEETHEART DEAL, **VCS** RECEIVED ALMOST ALL OF THE PROFITS FROM THEIR STRIPMINES.

OUTRAGED BY THIS ABUSE, THE HAITIAN PARLIAMENT VOTED UNANIMOUSLY FOR A MORATORIUM ON FURTHER MINING PERMITS.

BUT VCS STILL HOLDS RIGHTS TO MINING CONCESSIONS IN HAITI.

MEANWHILE, CONNECTED BUSINESSMEN CONTINUED TO REAP BENEFITS FROM THE RECONSTRUCTION EFFORTS.

DALBERG GLOBAL DEVELOPMENT, A CLINTON FOUNDATION CONTRIBUTOR, WAS AWARDED 1.5 MILLION TO IDENTIFY RELOCATION SITES FOR DISPLACED HAITIANS.

ROLLING STONE REPORTED, "IT BECAME CLEAR THAT THESE PEOPLE MAY NOT EVEN HAVE GOTTEN OUT OF THEIR SUVS."

LOOKS GOOD.

UH HUH.

GRANTS AND FUNDS TOTALING 138 MILLION WERE DISPERSED FOR TRANSITIONAL HOUSING.

ONLY 22% OF THE PROMISED SHELTERS WERE CONSTRUCTED.

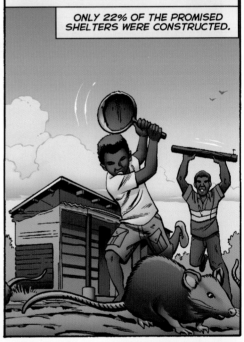

IN DECEMBER 2010, BILL AND HILLARY APPROVED A "NEW SETTLEMENT PROGRAM" OF PERMANENT HOMES.

TWO YEARS LATER, ONLY 900 OF THE CONTRACTED 15,000 HOMES HAD BEEN COMPLETED.

CLAYTON HOMES APPROACHED THE CLINTON FOUNDATION TO PROVIDE TEMPORARY HOUSING FOR HAITIAN SCHOOLCHILDREN.

THE COMPANY WAS STILL IN TROUBLE WITH FEMA FOR SENDING THOUSANDS OF SUB-STANDARD TRAILERS TO THE GULF COAST AFTER HURRICANE KATRINA.

THE TRAILERS SENT TO HAITI WERE OF MUCH THE SAME QUALITY.

THEY WERE NOT "HURRICANE PROOF" AS PROMISED AND WERE FILLED WITH TOXIC LEVELS OF FORMALDEHYDE AND BLACK MOLD.

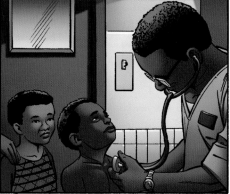

TRAILERS WERE ABANDONED AFTER HAITIAN CHILDREN BECAME SICK AFTER OCCUPYING THEM.

BACK IN CHAPPAQUA, BILL DREAMED OF A HOUSING EXPO IN HAITI.

BUILDING BACK BETTER COMMUNITIES

IT WOULD BRING DESIGNERS, ARCHITECTS AND CONTRACTORS TOGETHER IN PORT AU PRINCE.

THE GRAND PLAN FOR A HOUSING EXPO ONLY RESULTED IN THE CONSTRUCTION OF A FEW MODEL HOMES.

THEY PROVIDED SHELTER FOR SQUATTERS AND THE OCCASIONAL GOAT.

THE MOST AMBITIOUS PROJECT WAS THE MASSIVE CARACOL INDUSTRIAL PARK.

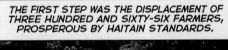

PARC INDUSTRIEL DE CARACOL

HONCHOED BY HILLARY'S RIGHT HAND AT STATE, CHERYL MILLS.

THE FIRST STEP WAS THE DISPLACEMENT OF THREE HUNDRED AND SIXTY-SIX FARMERS, PROSPEROUS BY HAITAIN STANDARDS.

THESE PROPERTIES ESCAPED THE RAVAGES OF THE EARTHQUAKE ONLY TO BE BROUGHT DOWN AS PART OF A RE-BUILDING EFFORT.

SAE-A, A SOUTH KOREAN CLOTHING GIANT WAS ENTICED TO BUILD AT CARACOL.

$124 MILLION WAS ALLOCATED, PLUS ANOTHER $100 PLEDGED TO THEM, FOR BUILDING COSTS THAT INCLUDED A POWER PLANT.

IN ADDITION TO A QUARTER BILLION DOLLARS IN AMERICAN TAX DOLLARS, **SAE-A** WOULD ALSO RECEIVE A FIFTEEN-YEAR TAX BREAK FROM THE HAITIAN GOVERNMENT.

AND THEIR GOODS WOULD ENTER THE USA TARIFF-FREE.

THE FACTORY OPENED WITH A CELEBRITY GALA.

DONNA KARAN

SEAN PENN

BEN STILLER

RICHARD BRANSON

HILLARY TOUTED IT AS A GREAT DAY FOR HAITI.

BILL TEARED UP.

BUT, AS BILL VASTINE OF THE **USAID** SHELTER TEAM SAID:

"IF THE AMERICAN PEOPLE SAW THE COST OF THIS, THEY'D SAY, 'YOU'VE GOT TO BE OUT OF YOUR MIND.'"

SAE-A

RATHER THAN THE HAITIAN PEOPLE, THE MAIN BENEFACTORS OF CARACOL WERE AMERICAN RETAIL OUTLETS.

DISCOUNT RETAILER

RETAIL★CORP

CLOTHING RETAILER

ALL OF WHOM WERE MAJOR CONTRIBUTORS TO EITHER THE CLINTON FOUNDATION OR HILLARY'S POLITICAL AMBITIONS.

CARACOL PROMISED TO EMPLOY 60,000 HAITIANS AND HOUSE MANY MORE.

IN THE END, ONLY FIVE THOUSAND JOBS WERE CREATED.

AND OF 25,000 PLANNED HOUSES, ONLY SIX THOUSAND WERE FINISHED.

THE PRICE OF THESE HOMES JUMPED FROM EIGHT THOUSAND TO 23,000 DOLLARS APIECE.

IN THE MEANTIME, THE STREETS OF PORT-AU-PRINCE ARE STILL POPULATED BY THOSE WHO SAW THEIR HOMES DESTROYED IN 2010.

THEIR NET WORTH HAS NOT CHANGED.

BUT THAT OF THE CLINTONS AND THEIR ASSOCIATES SURELY HAS.

QUID PRO QUO

A PATTERN OF BEHAVIOR HAS EMERGED.

A SERIES OF EVENTS THAT *ARE NOT MERE HAPPEN-STANCE OR COINCIDENCE.*

THESE ARE NOT BOOK-KEEPING ERRORS, OR SIMPLE MISTAKES.

YOU SHOULDN'T HAVE.

AND THE PATTERN REPEATS AGAIN AND AGAIN.

A PATTERN OF ASSOCIATIONS, DECISIONS, POLITICAL DETERMINATIONS AND, MOST OF ALL, PAYMENTS.

LOOK WHAT I FOUND AT OUR DOOR!

QUID PRO QUO

THE PATTERN BEGINS WITH A POOR COUNTRY THAT'S RICH IN NATURAL RESOURCES.

THE COUNTRY MUST BE RUN BY A TYRANNICAL AUTOCRAT WILLING TO DO BUSINESS.

BILL CLINTON ARRIVES WITH ONE OF HIS BUSINESS ASSOCIATES.

MEETINGS ARE HAD. DEALS ARE STRUCK.

BILL IS INVITED TO THAT SAME COUNTRY TO GIVE SPEECHES FOR EXORBITANT FEES.

HILLARY (IN WHATEVER POSITION SHE HOLDS) TAKES A FIRM STAND AGAINST ALLOWING THE COUNTRY IN QUESTION TO TRADE WITH AMERICAN INTERESTS.

AS THE DEADLINE FOR ANY DEAL DRAWS CLOSER, SHE EITHER GOES SILENT OR SUGGESTS HER POSITION MIGHT CHANGE.

HILLARY EVENTUALLY COMES AROUND TO REMOVE ANY RESTRICTIONS THAT ARE LEGAL OBSTACLES TO THE DEAL IN PROGRESS.

SHORTLY AFTERWARD, PARTICIPANTS IN THE DEAL WRITE CHECKS FOR THE CLINTON FOUNDATION.

AND WITH EACH STEP UPWARDS IN POWER AND INFLUENCE, THE FLOW OF CASH CONTINUES TO GROW.

THESE INCIDENTS REPRESENT AN UNDERGROUND ECONOMY OF WHAT SOME MAY CALL GRAFT HAPPENING RIGHT OUT IN THE OPEN.

AN ALLIANCE BETWEEN BUSINESS, POLITICS AND FOREIGN COUNTRIES.

QUID PRO QUO

BEHAVIORS SUCH AS THESE ARE BECOMING BUSINESS-AS-USUAL IN OUR HALLS OF POWER.

INFLUENCE PEDDLING AND CRONYISM ARE VISIBLE EVERYWHERE.

HOW ELSE TO EXPLAIN HOW A MAN OF LIMITED MEANS...

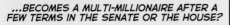
...BECOMES A MULTI-MILLIONAIRE AFTER A FEW TERMS IN THE SENATE OR THE HOUSE?

OR HOW THE CLINTONS WENT FROM THIS...

WE HAD NO MONEY WHEN WE GOT THERE AND WE STRUGGLED TO, YOU KNOW, PIECE TOGETHER THE RESOURCES FOR MORTGAGES, FOR HOUSES, FOR CHELSEA'S EDUCATION. YOU KNOW, IT WAS NOT EASY.

...TO OVER-SEEING AN INTERNATIONAL ORGANIZATION THAT TAKES IN BILLIONS OF DOLLARS FROM DONORS ALL OVER THE WORLD.

AND VERY LITTLE OF THOSE FUNDS SEEM TO FIND THEIR WAY TO THOSE THE FOUNDATION PROFESSES TO HELP.

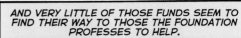

I FEEL YOUR PAIN.

CLINTON
CASH

A GRAPHIC NOVEL

THE CREATORS

Peter Schweizer is the author of multiple *New York Times* bestselling books, including *Clinton Cash,* and a senior editor-at-large at Breitbart News Network. His reporting has been the basis for *60 Minutes* segments, as well as numerous articles in the *New York Times, Washington Post, Wall Street Journal,* and elsewhere.

Chuck Dixon is a graphic novel editor, writer and publisher. He has contributed over a thousand scripts to publishers like DC Comics, Marvel, Dark Horse, Hyperion and others featuring a range of characters from Batman to The Simpsons. His comic book adaption of J.R.R. Tolkien's *The Hobbit* is an international bestseller. He is the co-creator of the iconic Batman villain Bane, and a prolific writer for *G.I. Joe* and *A-Team* for IDW Publishing, *The Good, the Bad and the Ugly* for Dynamite, *The Simpsons* for Bongo Comics, and many creator-owned projects, including *Joe Frankenstein.* He is the co-publisher of a line of graphic novels based on the American Civil War and wrote the graphic novel adaption of Amity Schlaes' *The Forgotten Man: A New History of the Great Depression.* He is the author of two series of action novels, *Bad Times* and *Levon Cade.*

Brett R. Smith is a professional commercial artist working in the comic book industry as a color artist, a storyboard artist in the advertising industry, and a graphic artist for multiple clients. He holds a B.F.A. in Animation. Smith started in the commercial art field in 1995 as an in-house color artist for Chaos! Comics. Since then he has worked with a wide array of clients, including Marvel and DC Entertainment, Hasbro, Cartoon Network, McCann Erikson, BBDO, and Saatchi & Saatchi. Smith has contributed to multiple premier properties and licenses including, *The Avengers, Batman, Superman, GI Joe, Wolverine, Suicide Squad, Guardians of the Galaxy, Hulk,* Detective Comics, Heineken, Chase Bank, Miller Beer, Cheerios, Pillsbury, Birds Eye and many others.

THE CREATORS

Sergio Cariello is a Brazilian-American comic book artist. Since 1992, he produced work for Marvel Comics and DC Comics, as well as popular independent companies like CrossGen Comics and Dynamite Entertainment. Cariello began his career as a Bullpen Letterer at Marvel. He's penciled Daredevil, Spider-Man, Thor, Iron Man, Incredible Hulk, Avengers and Conan. Cariello has also penciled for Batman, Green Arrow, Superman, Daredevil, Azrael and many others at DC Comics. His other projects include *The Lone Ranger* for Dynamite Entertainment, which received a nomination for an Eisner Award and won Best Western Comic Book of the Year from True West Magazine. He also illustrated *The Iron Ghost* series published by Image Comics, *Crux* for Crossgen Comics, the classic bestseller *The Action Bible,* and on the series *The Christ* for Kingstone Media. Carriello also illustrates *Kingdom Games,* a series for a video game company.

Don Hudson is a penciler and inker for comics, graphic novels, and storyboards. He started as an intern at Marvel Comics in the 1980s and joined the Marvel Bullpen staff in 1988. He later worked as an Assistant Art Director for Valiant Comics in 1990. He has worked on dozens of Marvel, Valiant and DC titles, including *The Avengers, Web of Spiderman, Captain America, Daredevil, Green Lantern* and *Silver Surfer.* He has also worked on storyboards and revisions for Sony Television Animation.

Graham Nolan is an Inkpot Award-winning cartoonist best known for his long run on *Batman* in Detective Comics and as the designer and co-creator of the iconic Batman villain, Bane. Since 1983, Nolan has worked in the comic book industry as a penciler, inker, writer and publisher, as well as an illustrator on the syndicated newspaper strips, *The Phantom* and *Rex Morgan, M.D.* He is also the creator of the graphic novel *Monster Island,* web-comic *Sunshine State* and the co-creator of the IDW horror adventure series *Joe Frankenstein.*

THE CREATORS

Paul Rivoche is a Toronto-based comic book artist, illustrator, and animation background designer. He illustrated a series of *Iron Man* covers for Marvel, a two-page spread for the Eisner Award-winning anthology *Little Nemo: Dream Another Dream* from Locust Moon Press, and art for the New York Times bestselling 294-page graphic novel adaptation of Amity Shlaes' *The Forgotten Man: A New History of the Great Depression.* Rivoche won both Gold and Silver awards in the Graphic Novel category of the LA Society of Illustrators' Illustration West 53rd competition.

Taylor Esposito is a comic book lettering professional and owner of Ghost Glyph Studios. As a staff letterer at DC, he lettered titles such as *Red Hood and The Outlaws, Constantine, Bodies, CMYK,* and *New Suicide Squad.* Prior to this, Taylor was credited on numerous titles for Marvel as a production artist. He is currently working on a new batch of creator-owned titles, such as *Gamer Girl and Vixen, Jade Street Protection Services* (Black Mask) and *Interceptor* (Heavy Metal Comics). Other publishers he has worked with include Rosy Press *(Fresh Romance/School Spirit),* Zenescope *(Grimm Fairy Tales),* and Dynamite *(Six Million Dollar Man: Fall of Man).*

Stephen K. Bannon is the Executive Chairman of the Breitbart News Network, LLC and Chairman of the Government Accountability Institute. A former naval officer, he is also an award-winning filmmaker and the host of Breitbart News Daily on Sirius XM.

THE CREATORS

Dan Fleuette is a writer and film producer. He began an art career at Otis College of Art and Design in Los Angeles with a dream of creating underground graphic novels. He quickly realized he did not have the patience to sit in one place and draw for hours on end, so he shifted to film production. After writing and producing over a dozen feature documentaries, he is happily back where he started—creating graphic novels.

Larry Solov is President and CEO of Breitbart News Network, LLC. Prior to joining Breitbart, he was a partner with the law firm of Katten Muchin Rosenman LLP. Mr. Solov graduated *Phi Beta Kappa* from Stanford University with a degree in Religious Studies, and from UCLA School of Law.

After a decade on the radio, **Eric Eggers** has built a reputation for his distinct voice, media expertise, and peerless research and messaging skills. Eggers' ghostwritten articles have garnered Drudge Report headlines, and his scriptwriting work has become the basis for Fox News one-hour specials. Eggers has worked on ghostwriting projects for national media celebrities and *New York Times* bestselling authors. Eric attended Florida State University, where he graduated with a degree in Creative Writing. He lives in Tallahassee with his wife and children.

ACKNOWLEDGMENTS

God is definitely on the top of my list. Without Him, we wouldn't be! Then, Celia Cariello, my mom, who supported my dream of becoming a cartoonist. George Theis for providing the bridge to my migration to the USA. My brother Octavio Cariello for opening a door for my first North American publication as an artist. My wife Luzia Cariello for helping me tremendously in building up my career—a constant helper in every way! Joe Kubert, for accepting me in his school, where all kinds of doors were opened for me. One job led to another, springing numerous new friends in this crazy business. Among those—Chuck Dixon, with whom I had the privilege of working on so many fun projects, including this one you hold in your hands! I cannot forget to thank Brett Smith and the A Team. I'm really proud to be a part of it. And lastly, ironically, all the real characters of this book! Without their infamous deeds, we would not have a story to tell, right?

- Sergio Cariello

I would like to thank my Rock of Gibraltar...my wife, Julia.

- Graham Nolan

I would like to first offer my sincere thanks to my Mom, Dad, Sharon and Frank for their love and support. I would also like to thank Steve, Dan and Peter for the opportunity and for their trust. Huge thanks to my creative team: Chuck, Sergio, Don, Graham, Paul, Taylor, Andy, Matthew and Alan, aka 'The A-Team', for kicking ass and taking names. Very special thanks to Lisa De Pasquale for her instrumental help and support. And last but not least I would like to express my deepest gratitude to God.

- Brett R. Smith